The Ten Commandments

Then And Now

James C. Lewis

The Spiritual Resources Foundation
3021 S. University Blvd.
Denver, Colorado 80210

Bible quotations are from the King James version

3/91

Quotations from EVERYDAY LIFE IN ANCIENT GREECE,
1977 edition, by C. E. Robinson, are used
by permission of OXFORD UNIVERSITY PRESS.

ISBN: 0-942482-07-7
Library of Congress Card Catalogue: 84-50912

TABLE OF CONTENTS

Other Books By The Author:

Positive Thoughts for Successful Living

Mystical Teachings of Christianity

Reincarnation and Translation (booklet)

How To Think Like A Winner

The Great Commitment

Finding The Treasure Within You

The Upward Path

The Spiritual Gospel

The Twelve Thrones

*All Things Made New
(To be published in 1985)

The First Commandment

*Thou Shalt Have
None Other Gods Before Me.*

De. 5:7

There are two versions of the commandments recorded in the Bible. One version is in Exodus 20: 3-17 and the other in Deuteronomy 5: 7-21. Although the Exodus version is the one that is most familiar to many people, the version in Deuteronomy is the oldest or, we might say, the first. We must keep in mind that the books of the Bible are not in order of their time of writing. Not even the chapters are in historical order. For example, the second chapter of Genesis was written some 400 years before the first chapter. These two chapters describe two different stories of creation. Bible scholars today tell us that there are many authors and editors who have played an important part in the production of the Pentateuch which has been traditionally attributed to Moses. In fact four different strands of material have been identified in the Old Testament and they are classified as J, E, P, and D, letters which identify either the name used for God or the priestly interest or the deuteronomic interests of the writer.

As you read the many stories in the Old Testament you will find many contradictions of information and the telling of the stories more than once giving different details. This does not imply that the great ideas seeking to be presented are false. It is only to suggest that we must do more than think of them as actual history and get into a conflict trying to make a historical harmony of the stories. Take, for example, the story of Noah and the Flood. One time it states he was to take two of each species of animals into the ark and another time seven of each species. Stories are told to consolidate a long oral tradition and are not told to give accurate historical information.

According to the story of Moses, he led the people out of Egypt. One day he was led to go up Mt. Sinai where God revealed to him the Laws by which the Hebrews were to live. There is quite a bit of drama connected with the giving of the law. As you read the story you will find that Moses must have been in good physical condition, for he was running up and down that mountain many times. Another version of the story even states that it was Mt. Horeb. One time Moses was gone so long that the people got impatient waiting for a word from God which they expected him to bring down and they began complaining to Moses' brother, Aaron. He got the people to turn in all their gold rings and earrings and other items of gold. He melted these down and out of it came a golden calf which they began to worship.

While they were doing that, Moses was supposed to be receiving the Commandments from God. The Commandments were written by the finger of God on two tables of stone. When God found out what the people were doing in worshipping the golden calf he was very angry and wanted to destroy them. But Moses interceded for the people and got God to change His mind. When Moses came down from the mountain he became very angry over the very thing that God got angry over and he destroyed the tables of stone and took some drastic measures to insure that this would never happen again. He called in some of the Levites, had them take their swords and they killed some 3,000 people who had taken part in this episode. Not to be outdone by Moses, God then caused a plague that killed many more.

Later Moses went back up the mountain and received a new set of tables with the Commandments written on them. These Commandments are referred to as the Decalogue, which simply means Ten Words. It would have been quite a feat to get all the information contained in the Commandments as we have them on two tables of stone.

Actually, it is believed by Biblical scholars that these laws or commandments are a product of a longer period of time. There are over 600 laws. There are 365 do nots and 248 dos. The Ten Commandments are only a few of the important ones.

If you have thought as I have, you may have made the same mistake I did in thinking that the first Commandment was "Thou shalt love the Lord thy God with all thy heart, and with all thy soul, and with all thy mind, and with all thy strength." (Mark 12:30) But this is not the first Commandment. This is a statement made by Jesus. A scribe came to Him one day and asked Him which is the greatest of all the commandments. No doubt he was thinking of the 613. It was to the scribe that Jesus gave the summary of the commandments that I have just quoted. The scribe had asked, "Which commandment is the first of all?" By this he meant which is first in importance. Jesus no doubt knew the Ten Commandments and many of the others. He was constantly in hot water with the religious leaders for violating them. Jesus was telling this scribe that loving God totally is the most important of all the commandments. He also said that the second was, "Love your neighbor as yourself." You and I know that this is not the second commandment. But again, Jesus was not quoting or attempting to refer to the basic ten; He was referring to the whole law code.

There were laws covering just about every action of daily living. Many of these laws were given specifically to keep the people from mixing with their pagan neighbors and taking up some of their practices and worshipping their gods. There were laws covering the worship of God and the offering of sacrifices for sins that were committed. Probably no one could keep all the laws perfectly. Most people probably did not even know what all of them were. So it would be impossible not to sin. There were varying degrees of penalties for violating the laws. Sacrifices made in the Temple were no doubt the most popular ways provided and this provided support for the Temple priests and the Temple.

The first commandment is this: THOU SHALT HAVE NONE OTHER GODS BEFORE ME." (De. 5:7) When the Hebrews came into the land of Canaan they were not monotheists. Their God was a war God. They believed that there were many gods but they gave their loyalty, or they were supposed to give their loyalty and worship, only to Yahweh. When they began settling down in Canaan they began worshipping the fertility gods of the Canaanites. Even before this time they worshipped many other gods. This Commandment therefore demanded that loyalty be given only to Yahweh. He was their God that brought them out of the land of Egypt. He fought their battles for them. He was the only one of the many gods that they were to worship. This type of loyalty and worship is considered to be Henotheism. It wasn't until much later that the Hebrews developed into strict monotheists believing that there was only one God of all people and of all nations.

But what does the Commandment mean for us today? We do not believe in many gods as they did. We believe there is only one God who created everyone. Yet in a way we do have the belief in many gods. A "god" is anything to which we attribute power. If we believe that our power to get things, to have happiness, to be healed is due only to some outer material object, then we are worshipping a false god. If we believe that someone can take our good from us we are making a false god out of that person. Money is often used as an illustration of a false god because it seems that we can get all the good things of life when we have enough of it. Also it seems that money is the thing that we go after with the most enthusiasm and the thing we think about the most in our daily lives. If we have it we are happy as a general rule. If we do not have it we are miserable and unhappy and begin plotting and planning on how we can get it. Many times we seek money because we think it will solve our many problems, give us independence, freedom, fame, and success. But money of itself can do none of these things. Money is not evil even though there are individuals who misquote the Bible and say that money is the root of all evil. What the Bible actually says is that the love of money is the root of all evil. Money is neither good or bad. It is a medium of exchange that makes our daily living a lot simpler than it would be otherwise.

However, we should not make a god out of money. The Commandment says that we should have no other gods before the one God. First priority should be to seek the Lord, the Lord God that is within us. This Lord God is sometimes referred to as our Real Self. It is the God-Self that is created in the image and likeness of God and that is eternal, unchanging, and totally perfect. Only a strong conscious relationship with this inner Lord can make you happy and me happy. We must be willing to put aside the worship of the god of personal desire and personal ambition. We must let the Lord be our guide. Instead of us telling God what we want Him to do for us we need to let God tell us what is best for us.

There are many unfortunate people who do not even know there is a Lord God within them. They are living in the darkness of human ego consciousness. They seek, search, strive, and often fight to get the material things of this world. I read in the paper recently a sad story of a young boy who killed his mother. He felt neglected by her and was actually neglected by her because she was so intent on making something of her life. Found among some of her writings was a goal list that she had made. I believe the article said there was only one reference to her son on the list. She also states that she refused to let anything into her mind that would take her away from seeking after her goals. What a tragedy. It is unfortunate that today there are many metaphysical teachers who advocate this type of goal seeking after material things and after success, fame, and fortune. They have not learned yet that the things in the outer world are attracted to us and not sought after when we are working with our indwelling Lord. Jesus said, find the inner kingdom and those outer things will be added to you and they will be added in abundance. He told of how God provided for the birds. He described the blessings as being greater than Solomon and all his glory.

However, the requirement is this. We must put God first in our lives. We can have no outer gods before this inner God. We just seek the guidance of the inner Lord and not let our personal gods carry us away on false and futile side trips that lead to misery and despair and defeat. We must make a commitment to the Lord of our Being and it has to be one of unquestioning loyalty.

There is another god that has made his appearance on the human scene today that we must be careful of and he is the computer god. He is a lot of fun and it seems that he is awfully smart. It seems that he can solve all our problems. But he cannot solve all your problems. He cannot even solve the ones that are most important to you right now. He can do some wonderful things for you but he can never replace the one, true intelligent God within you. He cannot match you up with the right person or tell you what type of work you should be involved in. He cannot tell you where you should live. He cannot tell you how much creative potential you have or even express that potential for you. Only the Lord God within you can give you these important answers. We should not expect more from computers than they can give. They are a blessing and can be of great benefit but we should not worship them.

There are many gods in our culture today and we have to be very careful that we do not get carried away by an unconscious or even a conscious worship of these gods. The Greek historian, C. E. Robinson, made this important statement in his book on the history of ancient Greece. He said, "In all spheres of life — religious, artistic, educational and the rest —stagnation of the human spirit sets in when Means are mistaken for Ends, when ritualism, for example, is made a substitute for worship, when technical skills take precedence over the search for beauty, or when pedantry obscures the true appreciation of literature. No age can escape the temptation; but in a scientific age the temptation is perhaps strongest of all.

The opportunities which Science holds out are so dazzling that it seems fatally easy to think them desirable in themselves. Yet obviously it is the use to which they are put that determines their value. The very same means which, if rightly used, may carry us into Utopia, might equally land us in the nightmare robotism of some Brave New World."

Robinson was seeking to describe the Greek spirit and interests. They were more interested in the developing of the mind. Wealth was to enable them to have time to enrich their minds by searching for truth. Robinson further states, "They (the Greeks) were athletic, none more so; but their spare time was devoted to the exercise of mind, perhaps even more than of body, so that their word leisure or 'schole' took on the meaning of 'school.' " When we hear the word gymnasium we think of it as an athletic club. To the Greeks it was much more than that. It was a place for developing the mind with the search for truth as well as a place for exercising and developing the body.

I like to think of our Unity Church as a gymnasium in this way. We exercise the mind. We search for truth no matter how shocking its discovery may be. We search for the Lord. We seek to put the inner Lord first in all that we do. We seek to enrich our minds through study and therefore offer many classes where people can come who are interested in cultivating or developing their soul consciousness. We seek to cultivate the soul with truth ideas. We also have the Yoga classes, four a week, that are highly beneficial in the developing of the body. There are others that we would like to have and perhaps one day we will evolve to the point where we can have many more classes.

We also believe the summary of the Mosaic law, given by Jesus, to be most important. To love the Lord with all our mind, strength and soul is most important. This inner Lord is your only real security. He is your help in every need. He will never reject you for any reason. You cannot shock Him by any past action or confession. He already knows what you are, what you have done, and He even knows what you are contemplating or attempting to do. Many of the things you might be thinking about He knows will only lead to disaster. Therefore He is ready and prepared to give you certain and sure guidance. His only desire is to help you to express your real, true and great potential. He wants you to enjoy creative living. However, we must be willing to put aside our false gods. This does not mean that we live isolated or ascetic lives. But it does mean that we put first things first. Seek the enrichment of the mind through the study of spiritual truth. Also seek the spiritual development of the soul through times of communion and listening to your God who is within you.

The Second Commandment

*Thou Shalt Not Make
Thee Any Graven Image.*

De. 5:8

As we continue to study the commandments we must constantly keep in mind that these are primitive peoples. They had little or no scientific knowledge of their world. They attributed causes of outer phenomena to spirits or gods. They believed these spirits could be placated to do their bidding. They believed in magic and they were highly superstitious. They believed they were exclusive; that their God was the most important of all the gods. They believed that even the gods had fights and arguments. The Hebrews were not the only ones who believed this. The Greeks also believed they were exclusive. If you were not a complete Greek, both parents Greek, then you were a second class citizen.

The Hebrews believed they had a special covenant and agreement with their God, Yahweh. The Ten Commandments are only a small portion of the complete Law Code by which they were supposed to live. It was also a Code that would bind the twelve tribes into a harmonious and cohesive unit.

The commandment against making graven images was for one purpose: to keep the people from worshipping other gods. The graven image was an image carved from stone, metal or wood. There were also molten images that they made and worshipped. There is a story about Micah who must have been connected with some local shrine. His mother made an image

out of 200 pieces of silver for him. She said, "I had wholly
dedicated the silver unto the Lord from my hand for my son,
to make a graven image and a molten image." (Judges 17:3)
She also gave him an ephod and a teraphim. The ephod was a
garment that the priest wore in performing the rituals at the
shrine. At this time of their history there was no Temple at
Jerusalem. The teraphim was a household image that the
people would worship.

You may recall the story of Jacob and Rachel that brings
out even more clearly how much image worship was a part of
Hebrew religion. When Jacob decided to return home after
serving his father-in-law Laban for some fourteen years, he
gathered together his family and left one day while his father-
in-law was away. When Laban returned and found they were
gone, he took off after them. When Jacob saw him coming he
was quite concerned. The father was upset but not because
Jacob was leaving with his daughters. The father was upset
because his household gods were missing. He wanted to search
the caravan to see if Jacob had stolen his gods. He went
through the caravan searching everything and everyone. When
he got to his daughter Rachel she said she was not feeling too
well. The Bible expresses it by saying she was "in the way of
woman." She was lying to her father. She was really sitting on
his household images of the gods. He excused her and
therefore she got away with the theft. Rachel believed that
having the images would guarantee her and her family success
and that she would inherit her father's wealth.

There is another interesting account of image making and
worship that is especially significant, for it was done by none
other than Moses himself. When the people were wandering in
the wilderness during the forty year period after they escaped
fom Egypt they had a unique problem that occurred. God got
angry with them and sent down some fiery serpents to bite
them. Many of the people died from the bites. They believed
they must have done something wrong, and they had, so they
went to Moses and told him they would repent and asked him
to pray for them. Moses prayed to God and he says that God

told him to make a bronze serpent and set it on a pole. When someone was bitten by one of the serpents he would look at the bronze serpent on the pole and he would be healed.

The graven images that were made were sometimes in the form of animals such as the golden calf that Aaron made. Some were in the form of birds and some in human form. The question we must ask is, "What was the reason for this commandment in a primitive community?" One reason for it was to reinforce the basic concept of obedience to the Lord. This was a big spiritual step. Instead of manipulating the god, the law stressed obedience to God. Primitives believed they could control God if they could see him. The control would be through ritualistic magical means.

This attitude of wanting to control God and get Him to do what we want Him to do survives even today in Christianity, such as the performing of rituals to guarantee one will not die without the assurance of going to heaven. We have many images in the form of carved statues of individuals who are supposed to have power to help us mortals left on earth. Some even believe they can get God to make it rain or not rain if there is too much already. Even in Unity we have said for years a prayer for weather conditions. Weather is controlled by mass, collective consciousness and not by some god of weather. Of course the prayer for weather conditions was for the purpose of trying to establish a harmonious weather and was not for the purpose of placating or manipulating God.

So the second commandment is basically a prohibition against trying to exercise control over God. God is to be known for the Hebrew through His actions and not through material forms. He is the God that brought them out of the land of Egypt, the invisible God that spoke to Moses on the mount. It is not only a prohibition of trying to make an image of Yahweh but also not to make images of the other gods that they believed existed.

What spiritual meaning is there for us today in this commandment? We must go a little deeper than the surface meaning. We must seek the deeper level of principle in order to have this commandment make sense for us today. In our day we are, or at least many people are, aware of the great influence of the mind in the process of manifesting outer phenomena. We know that certain images held in mind manifest in our lives — constructive images manifesting something good and negative images manifesting something undesirable. We also know that many of the images that we would like to manifest, do not. In fact it almost seems that the ones we do not want to manifest do and the ones we do want to manifest do not. The Apostle Paul experienced the frustration of this when he said, "For that which I do I allow not: for what I would, that do I not; but what I hate, that do I." (Rom. 7:15)

What is the cause of this phenomena of human nature? The answer is quite complex but it is also very simple. What we do not want, what we fear, resent, hate or detest is backed up with a lot of negative feeling and negative expectancy. In other words we hold a negative image in our conscious minds. This does not necessarily have to be a "visual" image. It can simply be negative thought, some negative attitude or concept. This negative image arouses in us negative feelings or emotions. The intensity of the feeling depends upon how seriously we think about the negative concept or image that we have in our minds. It depends upon what the problem is. For example if a person is filled with resentment and hate it can be a simple feeling of hate or it can be a very strong and passionate feeling that leads to drastic action. The simple feeling he may be able to suppress.

However, the point is this. A conscious image held in mind backed up with a corresponding, complimentary feeling is the combination that brings about some manifestation in our lives.

Now let us consider this from the positive point of view. There may be some good thing that we would like to have in our lives. Consciously we may want a home, car, companion, job, money, travel, or some other good that gets us excited on the conscious, intellectual level. However, what we do want is not usually backed up on the unconscious level with strong feelings of expectancy. In fact, you no doubt have heard many people say, "It is too good to be true for me." Or they may say, "I would like to do so and so" and then say with a very negative and discouraging feeling, "But I can't." Or they may express the negative feeling about the good they would like to have by saying they don't have the money, talent, ability, or even that God doesn't want them to have it. On the conscious level they want healing but feel that their condition is too serious or that it is even incurable. They may want and need supply for their needs but feel they are a victim of economic changes or bad luck.

It seems that on the human level it is much easier to arouse strong feeling about negative things than it is to arouse strong feelings about good things. So, therefore, when the strong feeling is absent in regards to the good that we want we do not get the manifestation.

The making of images in consciousness relates to this commandment. It is more a statement of principle. God does not force us to make any particular type of image because he left us free to follow His good guidance or to go off on our own. But the commandment is stating to us this important truth: "WHAT YOU CARVE OUT IN CONSCIOUSNESS WITH THE TOOLS OF THOUGHT AND FEELING IS WHAT YOU WILL MANIFEST IN YOUR LIFE."

This is not just a conscious process. Most of the image carving is going on in us on the unconscious level. Generally a person spends very little conscious time seeking to develop positive and constructive images. He gets so busy working or playing or fussing and arguing that little constructive imagery or positive and constructive thinking takes place. What we think about all through the day is contributing to the making of images in our consciousness. Here again I would like to stress that image making is thought and feeling and not just visualization.

Now we have to explain another perplexing problem that happens in this process of image making. It seems to the individual that many things happen in his life that have no relationship to the way he is thinking. He cannot see cause and effect relationships. The reason for this is that many manifestations that take place in our lives are due to images that have been formed and accepted in the unconscious phase of mind many, many years ago. And if you can accept it, it is very possible that a person is manifesting images that have been formed in previous life times. The graven images of a lifetime or even many lifetimes are doing their work. These unconscious images are more powerful, or at least seem to be more powerful, than the personal conscious images that we try to manifest. These unconscious images are backed up by strong feeling and when we try to change them on the conscious level we find that it is very challenging and quite often very difficult.

For example suppose a person seeks to change a habit. Consciously he may want to be free but it may take some effort to convince the unconscious that it can be free. The unconscious seems even to enjoy the negative image. Take for example the habit of smoking. When one begins to smoke he may think it is going to be something pleasurable, fashionable, or just something to do. When he begins on the conscious level it may make him ill to smoke but he gets determined and continues to smoke. Then an interesting thing happens: it really does become a pleasurable experience. He no longer gets sick or gets headaches; now he enjoys the habit. But along comes modern science and tells him that smoking is not good for his health and he decides he wants to quit. So he makes a conscious decision that he will stop smoking. He may even get very dramatic and tell everyone he is going to stop. But the unconscious says, "Let's see you do it." The pleasure of the habit is so strong that a simple conscious decision is not enough to change the unconscious habit.

There is another thing that is important to remember when we consider this process of consciousness manifesting things in our lives. Once an image or belief has been accepted on the unconscious level it begins to work twenty-four hours a day to bring about its manifestation. The unconscious never sleeps. Long after the conscious mind has forgotten about something or has gone on to think about other things, the unconscious, retains what has been given it and works around the clock to bring forth the manifestation. The unconscious even works during our conscious waking hours. We can be doing one thing consciously while the unconscious is working on something totally opposite of what we are thinking about. Also to show the tremendous power and influence of the unconscious, it can do many things at the same time whereas it seems the conscious mind has to take one thing at a time.

The images in the unconscious mind therefore work for you while you are awake, asleep, while you are busy playing, working, or doing any number of things. It works even when a person is in a coma.

Many of the images, most of the thought of an untrained or unillumined person are negative. As we grow up we are trained to believe and accept concepts that are not true. We are filled with many superstitions, for example. This is especially true in religious belief. We believe things about God, ourselves, and the universe that are actually false and we believe them with strong feelings. We are often afraid to challenge these beliefs but we should remember that negative images, negative beliefs, even if they seem to be beneficial, actually produce negative manifestations in our lives. There is no need to be afraid to search for the truth. There is no need to be afraid to challenge our religious heritage. Martin Luther challenged the established tradition and he opened the door to necessary and important reforms in religious thought. We still need more of this today. We need it, not only in orthodox tradition but we also need it in the New Thought or metaphysical tradition.

The Commandments to the primitive peoples were given for the specific purpose of controlling the people in the Covenant Community. Many things are taught to us for the specific purpose of controlling us. How can we fulfill the spiritual requirements of this commandment? It is misused quite a bit in the metaphysical teaching of today. Individuals seek to make images of personal desires. We have been told that "if you can see it in your mind, image it, you can have it." This does work to a degree but only to a small degree. What is not always stressed is that you also have to take what goes along with the manifestation of the personal image. In the medical field this would be called the side effects.

The proper way for the spiritual method is to let your indwelling Spirit project on the screen of your mind the image or images that are right for you. This projection may come in many forms. It may come as visual image or it may come as a hunch or a subtle feeling. In order for this to happen we must release all our personal images. We must be totally receptive as far as possible. We must be willing to accept and obey. We must be willing to believe that the image that the indwelling Spirit projects on the screen of our mind is possible to manifest. It took me a whole year and two projections of this inner image for me to get to the place where I could accept what the Spirit was guiding me to do. My conscious mind was intent on manifesting other images and I was not willing to accept what was being projected from within. I had carved out graven images of things I thought I needed and things I wanted and things I wanted to do.

The human personal ego is not always eager to let go and let the Spirit take over. We think we can do a better job of planning our lives. We often even think that we can think and plan bigger things than God can plan for us. Our plans are usually for personal, sensory gratification and pleasure alone. God's plans are for our spiritual growth and spiritual self-mastery. This is where the great conflict comes in. We must one day ask ourselves what is more important in our lives. Is it more important to manifest images of things; is it more important to use the imagination to demonstrate wealth and success? Or is it important to grow up and mature spiritually? Which is more important, the development of character, the development of spiritual qualities that are eternal in the soul or demonstrating and trying to control outer things and people?

Socrates said that the development of the soul is the most important. He stressed that if one would develop spiritual qualities in the soul he would have the wealth, all the outer things that would be needed to live a good life. Jesus stressed this same point when He said we should seek the treasures in heaven, knowing that when we developed inwardly in the soul that the outer things would be provided.

We should make up our minds that we are going to let God form the images in our mind, that we are going to let God think through us. This is intuitive thinking and the famous scientist Einstein said it is the highest form of thinking a person can be involved in. This inner tutor or teacher, Jesus said, would lead us into all the truth. This inner teacher will tell us what books to read and study. It will tell us what teachers have something to offer us to help us grow, to challenge us. If we are reluctant to accept the challenge we are only delaying the time when we could be having a better life and enjoying the thrill and excitement of discovery of new truths about life.

If you really want to fulfill the spiritual requirements of this second commandment, then make it a practice to sit quietly each day and say, I WILL LET GOD FORM THE IMAGES IN MY MIND OF WHAT I SHOULD THINK, SAY, AND DO." Then learn to be patient. Learn to listen or be receptive. Develop the attitude of joyous, eager expectancy. Your ego will no doubt be disappointed on occasion or on many occasions. But the joy will come when you have accepted and see the benefits and blessings of following the inner guidance. What is projected on the screen of your mind from within may be challenging but remember you will always be equal to the challenge because you have God working with you and for you as you work with and for Him.

The Third Commandment

*Thou Shalt Not Take The Name
of The Lord Thy God in Vain:
For the Lord Will Not Hold Him Guiltless
That Taketh His Name in Vain.*

De. 5:11

This commandment has been interpreted literally to mean we are not to curse or swear using God's name. Cursing may be a crude habit but I doubt seriously if this commandment ever referred to this practice.

The Hebrews had many names that referred to their God. Which one of the names is the commandment referring to? And if we try to make this commandment a universal principle, which name of the many religious faiths would we use? The Hebrews used Elohim, Yahweh, Adonai, El Shaddai and many other names to refer to their God. They would not speak God's real name that was revealed to Moses; they would use a substitute. One of the most popular substitutes was Adonai which when translated into English gives us "Lord."

Some Christians think that God's name is Jehovah. But this name would have no meaning to the Hebrew, for it is a word that was put together out of necessity. The older Hebrew manuscripts of the Bible were written using only consonants. In the margin of these texts, when they wanted to refer to God they would use the word Adonai, for they did not want to profane God's name, the name revealed to Moses and expressed in the text as YHWH. Later, when the scriptures were written using the vowels as well as the consonants, the vowels of Adonai were used with YHWH to form the word Jehovah. So the word Jehovah is the result of a combination of consonants and vowels and is not necessarily God's name.

To the primitive mind the name of a person was very important. The name of a person was related to his very existence. Not to have a name would be the same as not having any existence. To have one's name come to an end with his death and not be carried on through his children meant that he ceased to exist. Not to exist was one of the greatest fears and anxieties of the primitive Jew. In the creation story the naming of everything by Adam was a part of the creative process, you might say a putting of the finishing touches on the process of creation.

There are many examples in the Bible, when we read it with this importance of the name, that illustrate how important the name was not only for his relationship with God but for his own existence. For example you might want to read about Saul and David's relationship in I Samuel 24-21. Saul was the first king of Israel. But he did not do a good job and Samuel said he would be replaced by David. Saul tried on a number of occasions to kill David but was never successful. He no doubt feared that when David came to power he would eliminate the family of Saul and this would be the end of his existence. Saul invited David to come and talk with him. He said to David, "Swear now therefore unto me by the Lord, that thou wilt not cut off my seed after me, and that thou wilt not destroy my name out of my father's house." This passage clearly reveals how important it was to Saul that his name continue on through his descendants and by this his very existence.

The writer of Psalm 83:4 also brings out the importance of the name when he states, "They have said, Come, and let us cut them off from being a nation; that the name of Israel may be no more in remembrance."

A person's name was associated with the essence of his very being. To know his name was to know him, not just his physical appearance, but to know him as he really is, to know his character, his personality, and all the other qualities of a psychological nature that we relate to a person. A modern example of this would be expressed in a statement that an angry person might make about someone when he says, "Don't even speak his name around me." The idea being that the very name brings to his mind and arouses in his feelings some very unpleasant views he has about the other person.

As we read through the Bible we find many occasions where an individual's name was changed as a result of some spiritual experience. Abram's name was changed to Abraham. His wife Sarai's name was changed to Sarah. Jacob's name was changed to Israel. These changes of the name revealed that some great change had taken place within that individual. He or she was no longer the same person.

The primitive also believed that knowing the name of a person or thing gave him power over that person or thing. This might be expressed in modern psychological thought when we say that when we get to know someone we can control him or persuade him or influence him in some way or another.

When we understand this primitive view about the name and consider the story of God revealing His name to Moses we can better understand the powerful significance of the Covenant made at this time between God and Israel. God was bound to Israel because He revealed His name to Moses. He was to be their God, their only God, and they were to be His people. Even if Israel violated covenant agreements, they were still God's people and God had the responsibility to bring about a reconciliation. He would never abandon them even though they went astray.

The third commandment was also given to prevent the misuse of the power of God's name in magical practices. The people were not to use this power for selfish purposes. They were to use the power to do the will of God, to be obedient to the divine purpose and plan.

The making of false oaths, seeking to make them binding and powerful through the use of God's name, was also forbidden. Making a false oath in this way could be deadly serious business. To do so was to admit a total disbelief in God, a lack of trust and respect for God. When an individual used God's name in a superficial, casual or trivial manner it was tantamount to denying the very existence of God.

We should keep in mind when we study these earlier cultures that the majority of the people could not read. Oral traditions were very important to them. They passed along their stories and history from generation to generation. The spoken word was important to them. They no doubt had very good memories. They relied heavily therefore upon the words a person spoke. It was important to be able to trust what one heard another saying. Swearing is usually an indication that a person is trying to convince or persuade rather than telling and revealing his own sincere conviction. The Greeks despised the practice of swearing. When Alexander came in contact with the Scythians he discovered that they had a high moral and ethical standard regarding the spoken word. They said, "We swear only by keeping our word." That is a mighty, powerful and advanced ethical principle. It would be great if all people believed this way today. It would be wonderful if everyone took that much pride in his word so that when he spoke his word another person could depend upon it, believe it, and trust in him completely. The Persians would not swear either. There is an Arab proverb that states, "Never swear, but let your words be yes and no." This sounds very similar to a statement Jesus made when He said, "Neither shalt thou swear by thy head, for thou canst not make one hair white or black. But let your communication be, yea, yea; nay, nay: and whatsoever is more than these cometh of evil." (Mat. 5:35 & 37).

Some people today casually swear. They try to reassure or convince someone that they will do something by relating it to God or something considered holy or very special or valuable to them or to the person they are trying to influence. It is probably because of their lack of sincerity and honesty that they feel they must go beyond the yea and nay and try all manner of swearing and promising, trying to get their way with someone. They will swear on their parent's head or grave or on the name Jesus Christ or some other cherished and valued object or person. Jesus is just reinforcing the idea that one should have the character to do what he says he will do. There is no need for all the other manipulating nonsense when one is honest, dependable and trustworthy. He is saying to us in so many words, "Don't swear or make oaths you do not intend to keep. Do not deceive another by swearing by something that is holy."

What meaning can we find in this commandment for today? First we must ask the question, "What is meant by God's name?" God is not a personality. God simply is. God is sometimes referred to as Being, the One Cause of all existence. We should keep in mind as we seek to comprehend the name of God that Existence, God, does not mean form. Existence means the essence or substance of all that is formed. All forms are the creation of man and this is true whether we know it or not and whether we understand the process of manifesting the real essence of God. We have the power to misuse the essence or the power of God.

To illustrate what I mean by essence and form let me use the example of a sculptor using his clay to make a bust of some famous person. The clay is the essence. The sculptor gives the form to the clay. The clay is the cause of the form's existence but the clay did not give the intent, the sculptor gave that, he used the clay to express what was in his mind. All forms in this physical world are manifestations of the One Essence. Unfortunately we have not realized how powerful we are in that we have been given freedom by God to use and express this One Essence in any way that we so choose.

In metaphysics we often hear the words "I Am" as being the name of God. This comes from the conversation Moses had with God on Mt. Sinai. The "I am that I am" statement is used to express the nature of God, to reinforce the name of God that was revealed to Moses as Yahweh. Yahweh means "to be, to come to pass." God is that which causes all things to be, to have existence. He causes all things to be but not by intent. Intent is the reaction of man. God never intended that His Essence ever be expressed in negative ways such as illness, poverty, wars, germs, or any other unpleasant manifestation. The words "I am that I am" mean something like, "I cause to be what is." This does not mean to imply that God wants things to be the way they are. In the example of the clay and sculptor, and this is a rather crude and very limited way of expressing it, the clay may not want to be expressed or formed as a bust, especially if it is the bust of some ugly human being. God does not want us to express the life force as sickness but because we are free, there is no alternative.

The "I Am" is also associated with Jesus. In the Gospel of John, Jesus made seven statements regarding the I AM. He said "I am the light of the world, the bread of life, the resurrection and the life" and other statements. Metaphysical teachers have therefore related the "I am" with the Real Self, the name of God within us. The "I Am" is the true "image and likeness of God" within each person. Most humans identify with a personal, human ego self. They form an image of who and what they are that is based upon information perceived through their senses. This information includes the values, beliefs, and traditions of the culture in which they are raised. It also includes attitudes regarding family relationships and genes and other biological factors. This image of the human self is therefore very limited. When we consider the negative religious beliefs that we have been taught about the human self we find that we have formed in our consciousness a very negative and false image of what we truly are.

Jesus came to help us correct that image. He stated to the people of the time, especially the religious leaders, that they were in essence "gods." Jesus did not even use the expression 'son of God' on this occasion, for he was quoting the Old Testament where the Psalmist says, "I have said, Ye are gods." (Ps. 82:6)

What we refer to as the son of God self is within every person regardless of his or her circumstances in life. Because of the many negative beliefs that many have they cannot conceive in their minds the possibility that they are something special. We cannot conceive what we have not perceived. Perception cannot be given to a person intellectually. It is only when the Real Self has the opportunity to make itself known that the individual experiences what is referred to as "enlightenment." That is the moment of true spiritual awakening. When that happens in an individual he should not use the power that comes through this realization for selfish purposes. He really does not need to but the human ego which has lived so long in lack, limitation, and frustration tends to get carried away and begins to want everything it can possibly get in the outer world of physical phenomena.

Those who are spiritually sincere would avoid this negative use and expression of the inner power, for it is the same as taking God's name in vain. The Psalmist caught a vision of the realization of power that comes when the Real Self, the God Self, makes Its Presence known in human consciousness. He states, "The Lord also will be a refuge for the oppressed, a refuge in times of trouble. And they that know thy name will put their trust in thee, for thou, Lord, hast not forsaken them that seek thee." (Psalm 9:9-10) This is a beautiful Psalm. He is saying in so many words that when we come into a conscious relationship with God, when we know His name in us, then we know where to put our faith and trust. This inner realization is a stronghold. It may be the only thing that we have to hold to in times of trouble and when we have problems that seem like mountains. But when we know the name of God, we know our relationship with Him, we know that He is all-powerful. We know too that He will never forsake us. Even when we give up in despair He does not forsake us. Knowing this should help us in our times of depression, frustration, and discouragement. When we maintain our trust in Him we will be lifted out of these negative emotions and we and our lives will be transformed.

To "know the name" is not just an intellectual knowing. It is a knowing with our whole being. It is the Real Self in union and harmony with the Universal Self, God. Those who know with their minds and hearts are aware of this devine relationship. And those who are truly aware would not use the power in vain.

The word *vain* means: "having no real value; worthless, unsuccessful; useless." So this commandment is really helping us to realize that it is useless and a waste of time to use the inner power just to get things in the physical world. There is nothing wrong with things in the physical world but they should not be the object of our existence. All things will be added, Jesus said, when we learn to use and express and follow the inner light. We should not use the power of the name, the consciousness of the inner power, to glorify the personal self. We should use it to the glory of God. We should let It express through us as Jesus suggested when He said, "Let your light shine." Do not try to take the outer light and impress it on the unconscious. This is the personal selfish light. Rather, let the unselfish, spiritual light from within reveal that which is right, good and true. Do not waste your time in useless pursuits, the pursuit of something you think will make you happy or solve a problem, but in many instances will only make things worse.

It has been suggested by many teachers that your ability to say "I Am" should not be used in a negative identification. In other words do not say, "I am sick" even if you are. Or do not say, "I am poor" even if it is a fact. Do not say, "I am afraid" even if you are shaking in your boots. Instead, be a positive and constructive thinker and say, "I am healed" or "I am rich." Doing this may work wonders for you or it may frustrate the devil out of you. Do not let yourself get caught in the guilt trap about it. Some people can say the I am statements in a positive way and not experience frustration. But some people cannot do this and they should not be made to feel that they are negative. A lot of the "I am" affirming is really only an effort to convince an unbelieving personal self. When Jesus said "I Am" He was stating or expressing what He knew He was. He knew He was the light of the world, a creative expression of the wisdom and intelligence of God. He knew He was the "bread of life." He knew that God always provided for all His needs. He knew that he was the resurrection and the life. He stated in the Garden that He had power over his body; that He could lay it down or take it up and that no one could take it from Him without His consent. He knew that life was eternal and deathless. Jesus was not seeking to become something, He knew He was all those things already.

We can say positive "I Am" statements until we are blue or purple in the face, but if the purpose is selfish, it is in vain, meaning useless and unsuccessful. If we are doing this trying to convince ourselves to believe something that the unconscious does not believe, we are wasting our time. However, if it is through a genuine realization in trust, then we do not even need to say it to try and persuade. We will then have that inner knowing that Jesus had when He said "I Am."

As one matures on the spiritual path he or she will have those wonderful realizations about the "I Am." There will be the realization in which the individual can truly say, "I do not have to try and claim or get anything, I am rich. I am rich-not because I have many things, but because I know that God is the One true, unlimited, and dependable Provider. I am secure in God." The personal "I" becomes identified with the spiritual "I Am" or the name of God, the One Presence. When this happens, the human ego, which is not bad, only misinformed, becomes free and is liberated from the influence of false beliefs. It comes out of its Babylonian Captivity. It gains a new lease on life. It discovers or feels an inner joy and happiness not based on things or outer relationships but a joy and happiness that is based on a relationship with God. The human ego becomes one with God and this is the ultimate purpose of life.

The Fourth Commandment

Keep the Sabbath Day,
To Sanctify It . . .

De. 5:12

There is much more descriptive material that has been added to this commandment. This Deuteronomic version is different from the Exodus version in that this version reminds the people of the convenant relationship made with them when they were freed from Egypt. It stresses the idea that they now have the opportunity to rest, for they are no longer slaves as they were in Egypt and had no opportunity to take a day off.

The Exodus version stresses the idea of rest but it does so from a more religious point of view. It refers to the rest that God took on the seventh day when He created the world and that the people should follow suit. This is a much later version and no doubt represents the attitude of the priestly interests.

The idea of the sabbath day did not originate with the Hebrews. In fact they probably adopted the practice from the many other cultures in which they became involved. They were nomads when they left Egypt and it would have been rather impossible for them to have such a strict law and follow it in their desert wanderings. Their flocks would have to be taken care of daily and other aspects of the code would have been useless or impossible to fulfill.

The meaning of the word "sabbath" is simply "to cease, to abstain, to terminate." They probably picked up this idea when they were captives in Babylon which began in 586 B.C. In Babylon the day was thought of as the "day of quieting the heart." The Babylonians also felt that the 7th, 14th, 21st, and

28th days of the month were evil days. They believed they had to stop all their normal activities because of the supernatural powers. They feared these spirits would harm them in some way if they did not pay some sort of recognition to them. They were not astronomers and you can see that their beliefs were related to lunar movements. Some people believe in this lunar influence even today.

The Kenites in Palestine thought of the 7th day as the "Day of Saturn." It was for them the star representing misfortune. This "black" god was worshipped by the Kenites and the Israelites. No lights were lit on that day for they did not want to offend or disturb the god.

Some scholars think that the sabbath was instituted by the prophet Ezekiel, the prophet of the Exile in Babylon, to compensate for the lunar festivals the Hebrews observed and may even have participated in. Why the seventh day? Because they learned in Babylon that the number seven was a sacred number.

The Sabbath is Saturday and not Sunday even though Christians seem to think Sunday is the sabbath. At least one Christian denomination takes the commandment rather literally and has its religious services on Saturday. They are the Seventh Day Adventists. They are right in that the sabbath is the seventh day. However, the practice of observing the sabbath on the first day has been related to the Creation of light in the story of Creation. And who was the "light of the world" in Christian belief? It is none other than Jesus. Also Jesus rose from the dead on Sunday. The first Christians were Jews and they no doubt continued to practice and adhere to many of their old beliefs. They would attend the synagogue meetings on the seventh day, the sabbath, and then go to some of the Christian meetings on Sunday. You will recall the meeting in the upper room on Pentecost day. There were no Christian churches as such at that time. The Jews who were interested in this new cult that was developing, called Christianity, would keep one foot in tradition and stick the other one out to see what was going on. Many still do this today in regards to their search for truth. They stay closely attached to tradition but they seek new ideas in the New Thought or Metaphysical churches.

Sunday came to be known to the early Christians as the Lord's Day. It is quite interesting to note that the commandment has been used by Christian leaders to make people feel obligated to attend church on Sunday. It has been and probably still is considered to be a serious offense when one does not attend church on Sunday. Yet the founder of Christianity, Jesus, would quite often violate the laws of the sabbath with His disciples.

The institution of the sabbath was just another way to control the people. There were very severe penalties for its violation. In Exodus 31:14 we read, "Ye shall keep the sabbath, for it is holy unto you: every one that defileth it shall surely be put to death: whosoever doeth any work therein, that soul shall be cut off from among his people." Death would have been serious enough but to the primitive mind to be cut off from among his people would probably be an even greater fear, for he would be excommunicated from the Covenant Community.

In Numbers, the 15th chapter, there is the story of a man who was simply going around gathering up pieces of wood on the sabbath. He was caught and was brought to Moses and Aaron to see what should be done about this violation of the sabbath. Moses evidently prayed and asked God how the man should be punished and we are told that God answered him saying, "And the Lord said unto Moses, The man shall be surely put to death; all the congregation shall stone him with stones without the camp.'" (Num. 15:35)

That is quite a severe consequence for picking up a few sticks of wood on the seventh day. This type of story reveals the primitive attitude and belief about God as being a very stern being. But it is probably more for the control of the people and it does not reveal the truth about the real character of God as love.

There is another reference about the sabbath that shows its connection with the Kenite belief and it is recorded in

Ex. 35:3. Remember I said that the Kenites would not light fires on the sabbath. Well, in this passage we are told that God spoke to Moses saying, "Ye shall kindle no fire throughout your habitations upon the sabbath day." Why would God want to be satisfied in this way? What kind of a God would it be that changed His mind, was sensitive to rejection, and demanded such simple and foolish requirements. There were many restrictions the people were to follow in order to try and keep the sabbath holy. In fact there were so many they could not possibly even remember all of them.

As I have said Jesus violated many of these restrictions. He healed on the sabbath and this was forbidden. He and His disciples were walking through the corn fields on the sabbath, picking the corn and this was probably a double violation, violating the "sabbath day's journey" and the prohibition against working by picking the corn.

Jesus probably violated the "sabbath day's journey" many times, for He constantly traveled about the countryside teaching and helping people. Josephus the Jewish historian says that the sabbath day's journey was probably about five or six furlongs. This would be from 3,031 to 3,637 feet. In other words the individual could not even walk our present day mile which is 5,280 feet.

Another computation of this distance was based on the incident of Joshua's crossing of the Jordan river when the Hebrews first came into the land of Canaan. In giving instructions for the crossing of the parted river he told the people to follow the Levitical priests who were carrying the ark and they were to stay behind the ark by a distance of 2,000 cubits. A cubit is the distance from the elbow to the end of the middle finger. So this amounted to approximately 3,000 to 3,600 feet, depending upon whether they used the Hellenistic or Roman form of measurements. The Egyptians would describe it as 1,000 double steps.

Jesus sought to bring about a change of attitude regarding the sabbath. He saw how ridiculous these prohibitions were. He saw that the sabbath was only a tool being used to control the people. He saw that it was a great stumbling block in the path of the individual's search for truth. It was used to make the individual feel guilty and fearful.

Jesus, you will recall, healed the man by the pool of Bethesda on the Sabbath and claimed God as His father. This was serious heresy. The Bible says regarding this experience, "Therefore the Jews sought the more to kill him, because he not only had broken the sabbath but said also that God was his Father, making himself equal with God." (John 5:18) Note that it says they wanted to kill him. This same attitude was carried over into Christianity and no doubt many were killed for violating not only the sabbath but other Church prohibitions.

We are told very specifically in Luke that Jesus said, "The Son of man is Lord also of the sabbath." (Luke 6:5) This means not only Jesus but all human beings are lord of the sabbath. That is, they are more important than the observance of ritualistic rules and regulations and practices. Mark expresses this idea about the sabbath in his gospel by saying that Jesus said, "The sabbath was made for man, and not man for the sabbath . . . "(Mark 2:27)

The story of Creation is not a true account of the physical creation of the world. God does not rest. God is not a superhuman being that works as humans work. God does not get tired. We should keep in mind that the stories about creation in the first few chapters of Genesis are creation myths. All cultures had their myths about how the world was created by some being or god. We should not let their primitive views keep us in bondage. Yet many are in bondage because they take these stories literally. The truth is you were not created in the beginning in the sense that out of nothing God formed or created you. You and I and every person in this universe has always existed. Even the newborn infant has existed before he came into this world in that small body. The Spirit and soul of every person is eternal and indestructible. The body may die but not the soul or the spirit. The soul can and does rebuild a body and this process has been going on for millions of years and will continue to go on for many more

millions of years. It will take many eons of time for most
people to reestablish their complete conscious relationship
with God as Jesus had that relationship. This may seem like a
strange and hard teaching but it is the truth. Following rituals
and observing man-made rules and regulations such as the
sabbath are of little value in helping us reestablish a conscious
relationship with God.

What possible meaning could the keeping of the sabbath
have for us today? For one thing our society is so constituted
that the day off on Sunday affords the individual the opportunity to seek further enlightenment by joining with others
who are seeking the truth. It gives the individual an opportunity to think about other things that are not related just to
the physical world. It gives the individual the opportunity to
contemplate and think about himself in a spiritual way, to seek
the meaning and purpose for his existence, to seek his true
purpose in life, to seek to understand his relationship with
God, to seek a new and more enlightening view about God.

If we are to grow in our spiritual understanding we must
be willing to let go of our traditional Jewish and Christian
views about the sabbath and about many other rituals and
practices and beliefs that we have been told are essential to
believe. In Unity we do not attend church on Sunday because
we have to; at least I never attended for that reason. I went
because I was hearing new ideas about God. I was hearing
things that made me feel better and hearing ideas explained
that made more sense than what I had been taught.

There is a spiritual significance when we look to the
deeper level of this commandment. As I have already said, the
word means "to cease, to abstain, to terminate, to be at an
end." Keeping the sabbath, allegorically interpreted, can mean
that this is a time when we cease all outer activity and all
human thought about that outer activity and seek to enter the
"holy of holies" that is within us. It is a time to seek spiritual
enlightenment. It is a time to prepare ourselves in consciousness so that God can guide and direct us. The soul must be
prepared to receive the awakening of truth. Many people are

having problems and difficulties in life simply because of the lack of light in the soul consciousness. They are filled with many false beliefs about life. They are influenced by superstitions and false religious concepts. They are controlled by their passions, for they have not learned to discipline and train their physical passions and appetites.

Jesus said many are searching for the truth but that few would find it. I am sure He meant that few would find it this time, in this incarnation. He was no doubt revealing the fact that it takes a long time for most of us to get to the point where we are open minded enough to consider the truth. Some people go to church once a week and believe this satisfies the soul's requirements for spiritual understanding. Some may go much less, maybe two or three times a year. I have even heard people almost in a bragging way state that they have not been in a church for years. When I hear talk like that I feel rather sad for them, for they do not know what they are missing. They do not realize that just being in the consciousness and presence of people who are seeking the light can be a tremendous uplifting experience for them. Many of these people use the excuse that they do not want to associate with the hypocrites that go to church. But that is just a big rationalization.

Some day these individuals will realize that there can be very positive and constructive benefits by attending church. In my beginning search for truth I was glad to go to church on Sunday. I was also glad to be able to go to classes at other times during the week. My soul was starved for the truth. I was glad that there were books on truth that I could read when I was not able to go to church. I thought of it as a privilege to be able to go to church. I was glad that I had the health to physically get there. I never thought of going to church as an obligation. I never even considered the false belief that God would get upset if I did not attend.

I was glad that there was a church to attend. I was glad that many people before me had taken the time to give of themselves and their money to build a church and to keep it going so that when my time came when I needed it and the truth that it was teaching, it was there. I want the church to continue. I want it to be here when others come to realize the tremendous blessing it can be in their lives. I support it not only with my time but with my financial resources. I give not to become rich and prosperous for myself. I give so that the organization can continue to function and operate and be here when those who need it are ready. I am not making these statements simply because I am a minister of a church. Even if I were not a minister I would continue to support a church that teaches the truth. I would love to be a part of an organization that had the courage to speak out and tell the truth. I was doing this before the thought of ever being a minister came to my consciousness.

There is another way that we can consider this commandment. We can think of it as a reminder that we need to cease all outer activity and thought about that activity and take time to go to the church within our own consciousness. Many spend much of their time searching for things in the outer world to make them happy and successful. Some day we must come to realize that things of themselves cannot do that. Plato, the Greek philosopher before the time of Jesus, expressed this idea when he said, "One must turn the eye from the perishing world to what is real and eternal . . . turn the eye of the soul to the light." The outer world is the perishing or changing world. By perishing he did not mean that it would cease to exist or come to some cataclysmic end. He was only stating the fact that when we consider our total being of spirit, soul, and body, only the spirit and soul are eternal right now. The body dies and unfortunately we give most of our thought and attention to it. The outer world is a constantly changing world and this will always be the case. Eternal, unchanging Reality cannot be found or realized in a world that changes. It is the inner world of spirit that never changes. Truth never changes. Reality, non-physical, immaterial Reality, never changes. Principle never changes. God never changes. Therefore security and certainty and peace of mind cannot be found in the world that changes, for you will never know when or how it will change; you will only know that it will change and that will keep you disturbed and no doubt in a state of apprehension.

This does not mean that the outer world is bad or should not be a part of our lives. It does not mean that we should try to escape from it. It only means that we should seek the inner Reality, for this gives us the power over the outer world and we will be able to deal with it and all its changes without going to pieces. If you want the ability to deal with this outer, unstable world you must first seek the inner light. When the soul comes in contact, or when it experiences illumination, or when it experiences the Presence, wonderful things happen in the individual and in his or her outer life. Plato gives a beautiful description of what it is like. There can be no doubt that he had the experience. He said, "There is no way of putting it into words. Acquaintance with it must come after a long period of close companionship, when suddenly, like a blaze kindled by a leaping spark, it is born in the soul . . . Then at last, in a flash, understanding blazes up and the mind as it exerts all its powers to the limit of human capacity is flooded with light."

When an individual has that experience the troubles of life cease to have overwhelming negative influence. The person may still have the troubles and may still have to struggle to meet them but they will not overpower him and eventually he will rise above them. The individual is happy in spite of his problems. He is confident and has courage in the face of the greatest challenge. He runs from no one or no thing or no situation. He knows that with God only harmonious solutions will come forth. It may not happen overnight but the growth in consciousness begins that will change him and his life. You will note that Plato said it may take a long period of time. This is because we usually are not persistent enough or we do not become determined enough or we are not disciplined enough to put forth the constant effort that is necessary to find and discover the truth. It is not always easy to overcome human inertia that is caused by our passions, appetites, our desire for ease and luxury, and pleasures of all kinds. None of these things are evil or bad but they can be extremely strong deterrents. It may be easier to lie in bed and sleep than to make ourselves get up and get with it, to go to church. I have often heard people say they were very glad they did make that effort because something happened in them when they were in church. It was the spiritual consciousness and the atmosphere, the association with like minded spiritual seekers after the light.

When we learn to enter the inner church we have a wonderful discovery. We find that many of the things of life that we saw as being difficult things to do, we do not have to do by ourselves. We realize that we have the greatest power in the universe to help us. We can say, "I do not have to do it, all I have to do is let God do it through me."

Jesus expressed it by saying that we should go within the closet of our minds. He said, "But thou, when thou prayest, enter into thy closet, and when thou hast shut thy door, pray to thy Father which is in secret; and thy Father which seeth in secret shall reward thee openly." (Mat. 6:6)

The observing of the sabbath, the time to cease, should be a daily experience. You are the Temple of God. Your mind is the closet. Cease the outer thought activity by closing the door. Do not let the human fears and thoughts come in. Do not even let the personal ones, the personal desires for some good come in. Do not even let concern about your loved ones come in. Remember, Jesus said the Father would reward or bless you openly. This means you will be shown your part to do in the outer and you can be sure that God will do His part. God can work in people and situations when and where you cannot work.

Remember the time of meditation. Observe the time of meditation. Keep it holy. Take it seriously. The greatest soul growth takes place in these quiet moments. Sure, the personal intellect may get bored. But keep right on seeking the companionship of the Spirit. There may be periods when it seems there is a void. But never forget, God is there all the time. One day we will have that constant, continuous abiding consciousness that Jesus called "oneness." He prayed that we would be at one with God to the same degree that He was one with God. We will not only know the Presence but we will feel it and live in it.

The Fifth Commandment

Honour Thy Father and Thy Mother,
As The Lord Thy God Hath Commanded Thee;
That Thy Days May Be Prolonged,
And That It May Go Well With Thee,
In The Land Which The Lord Thy God
Giveth Thee.

De. 5:16

As we continue to study the commandments we must constantly keep in mind that they were given in order to keep the people under control. The Hebrews thought of themselves as God's chosen people and it was important to them that they should not mix with their neighbors.

This fifth commandment has two specific purposes. For one it reinforced the authority of the parents over the children and this was a strong influence in keeping not only the family but the clan together. It would keep the sons and daughters in the religious fold, for they would not be allowed to go seek special benefits from the other gods, especially the Canaanite fertility gods.

The father was the supreme authority in the family, for this was a patriarchal society. The father could kill any member of his family if that member tried to entice him to give up his faith in Yahweh or tried to get him to worship the fertility spirits or any other spirit or god. You will recall that Abraham was prepared to kill his son Isaac for religious purposes. He thought God told him to offer his son as a sacrifice. You and I know today that God would never tell someone to kill anyone much less a son for any purpose. God does not have to be placated or honored in such horrible ways. It was Abraham's primitive thinking that made him think it was God telling him to do such a horrible thing.

The father demanded absolute obedience from his children. They were not to question his authority but meekly do whatever he demanded. If he caught his children bad-mouthing him he could put them to death and no questions would be asked. Death was a rather severe penalty for cursing the old man or calling him a "mean old goat" when the kid got angry at him for any reason. In Leviticus 20:9 we read about this power of the father, "For everyone that curseth his father or his mother shall be surely put to death: he hath cursed his father or his mother; his blood shall be upon him." That is a little more severe than taking the son behind the woodshed for a little training. At least he would come back alive. But in the olden days he could be carried out in a box. It may sound strange to our modern ears that a parent would want to kill his own children but it was a common practice in early Biblical times.

The father could even sell his daughter as a slave if he could not arrange for her to get married or if she was an embarrassment to him. It was especially severe if she was the daughter of a priest. We read about this in Lev. 21:9 where it says, "And the daughter of any priest, if she profane herself by playing the whore, she profaneth her father: she shall be burnt with fire." The usual method of killing was by stoning so this would seem to be even worse, burning alive.

You will recall that the mother also had power in the family next to the father. Sarah told Abraham to have an affair with her maid Hagar so that the family could continue to have existence. Remember they believed that they survived through their children so it was very important that Abraham or any other man to have a son. It was important for the mother also that she have a son so they would all be around when the Messiah came and restored the kingdom of Israel. Rebecca helped Jacob in the deception of his father Isaac. Jacob had stolen the birthright from Esau, and Sarah helped Jacob disguise his smooth skin by putting animal skins on him so that he would feel hairy like Esau. Isaac who was practically blind could not see that it was Jacob. Isaac said, "You feel like Esau but you smell like Jacob." He knew something was up but he gave the blessing anyway. Then Jacob had to flee and his mother was a part of all this human deception.

Another reason for this commandment was to protect the parents when they got too old to exercise human power over the children if they were rebellious. Not many parents lived to an old age but for those who did, it was often to their regret. The children would think nothing of sending their parents out into the wilderness where they were often eaten by wild animals or left to die of exposure. Some parents were even forced to kill themselves. The writer of the Proverbs refers to these attempts of the children to get rid of their aged parents when he writes, 'He that wasteth his father, and chaseth away his mother, is a son that causeth shame, and bringeth reproach." (Prov. 19:26)

When the Temple and the priesthood was in full operation the religious leaders needed money to keep the expensive operation going. They made up a special interpretation of the law whereby children could give any money that would be used to support their parents, to the temple as a gift to God and they could do this without violating the fifth commandment. Jesus rebuked the religious leaders for this practice, which was called "Corban."

Jesus also violated his commandment but it was not in a cruel way. When his mother came to get Him at Capernaum to give up His teaching there was such a large crowd around Jesus that she could not get to Him personally. She sent word through the crowd that she was there. Remember now that the mother as well as the father had supreme authority over the children. When Jesus got the message that she wanted Him to return home and quit causing trouble with His teaching, He should have been obedient and gone along with her. Instead Jesus asked the question, "Who is my mother? and who are my brethren?" (Mat. 12:48) Jesus did not wait for an answer but said, "For whosoever shall do the will of my Father which is in heaven, the same is my brother, and sister, and mother." (Mat. 12:58) In this passage Jesus was not referring to Joseph his father. He was referring to the inner Presence of God. This is the same God-Presence that is within everyone. In this incident Jesus is saying that we should not let the traditions of family ties and rules keep us from following the inner spiritual guidance.

The time comes in the life of every person when the individual will begin to take the first tentative steps toward seeking the truth. When this happens he cannot let family or religious affiliations hinder or stop him from seeking and following the guidance of Spirit. Jesus even went a little farther and expressed this idea more strongly on another occasion when He said, "If any man come to me, and hate not his father, and mother, and wife, and children, and brethren, and sisters, yea, and his own life also, he cannot be my disciple." (Luke 14:26) I do not believe Jesus meant to hate as we usually think of hate today. The Greek word from which the English is translated has other shades of meaning and it would seem that the translators would have used one of these other meanings. The Greek word is "miseo." It also means "to disregard or to be indifferent to." To be a disciple is to be a seeker after truth. Seeking the truth has to become the most important thing in our lives. Unfortunately only a few at a time will make this kind of a commitment. The majority let their parents persuade them to stay within the traditional framework. Or it may be that they are persuaded by their friends. Jesus did not hate His mother. You will recall that while He was on the cross He gave her over into the care and keeping of one of his disciples. However, Jesus had no intention of letting her fears and apprehensions stop Him from teaching the truth to as many as He could, even if it meant upsetting the religious leaders and her. Jesus had something important to do and that something was more important than family ties.

There is an even deeper spiritual meaning for us today in this commandment. To grasp this deeper meaning we must relate the commandment to ourselves. The spiritual meaning will have nothing to do with outer human relationships.

First we must ask, "Who is our father and who is our mother?" What is it that gives birth or expression to ideas and concepts in our soul consciousness? The father is the intellectual, conscious mind. It is that phase of the mind where we do our thinking, analyzing, judging, rationalizing. The mother is our feeling, emotional nature. It is the unconscious phase of the soul, the storehouse of memory and of all our beliefs, habits, and attitudes toward life and all expressions of life.

It is thought and feeling working together that gives expression to all the concepts born in the soul consciousness. Concepts are formed or "born" in two ways. The first way is through the senses. We are constantly receiving sensory input. We see things, we hear things, we taste, touch and smell things and from all this information we form concepts, beliefs, opinions, attitudes, habits in our soul consciousness based upon this outer information. The other way that we form concepts is based upon spiritual revelation. We receive knowledge of truth in the form of ideas from our own indwelling Presence of God. When these ideas come we think about them and form a concept or concepts based upon this higher information. However, our concept will be influenced by the beliefs and attitudes that we already hold in consciousness and therefore, in many instances, we will misinterpret the spiritual idea. This means that our concept will be less perfect than the pure idea. For example when the idea of the One God is revealed, we may give a human interpretation to it and the God will turn out to have many human characteristics.

As we "think on these things" either ideas from within or sensory input, we form concepts in the soul about ourselves, about God, and about the world we live in and all our human relationships. We develop in consciousness attitudes that

motivate us and beliefs that dictate our behaviour. We also
develop habits that control and in many instances overwhelm
us.

If we are to make progress in our spiritual growth we
cannot let sensory input into our thoughts and feelings guide
and direct us. To honor our inner parents we must let them
follow the truth rather than opinion or sensory information.
We must follow truth instead of religious tradition. We take
away the right of the father, the intellect, to kill new ideas, the
sons and daughters that are born as a result of our spiritual
seeking. We do not let the intellect dictate to us. We let the
Higher Power, God in us, do the dictating. Jesus called this
doing His father's will. In His case that father was not intellect
but the Spirit of God in Him. When we seek to follow the
inner light, the inner urge, we may meet with human opposition. This opposition may come from our own human parents.
I recall in my own experience that I had to meet it. My mother
and sister were not the least bit interested in the metaphysical
teaching that I had discovered and thought was so wonderful.
They thought it was horrible. I never once got a kind word of
approval from either of them. They both thought it was some
silly phase I was going through. They did not realize, especially
in the beginning, how serious I was about it. I loved both of
them but I could not let their negative disapproval keep me
from following my inner guidance. As a result I was totally
rejected by them. I have come to understand what Jesus meant
when He said that those who do the will of His Father were his
mother, sister, and brothers.

How many times over the years have I heard someone say,
"I love the truth but my wife or husband does not approve so I
go with her or him to their church in order to keep peace in
the family." I would only say to that type of thinking what
Jesus said about it. He said, "I came not to bring peace but a
sword." The sword is a symbol of truth. Jesus continued on by
saying this sword of truth would cause havoc in family
relationships and all human relationships. It would cause
havoc in both the outer human family and the inner family of
thoughts, feelings, beliefs, attitudes, and habits.

To follow the truth symbolized by the sword we would have to disregard all human attempts to keep us in line and to stay within the religious tradition that we were brought up in. We would have to disregard the guilt feelings that conscience uses to keep us in line. You have heard the expression, "Let your conscience be your guide." Well, when the spirit of truth comes forth in consciousness, we have to let it be our guide and disregard the human training represented by "conscience." Conscience can make us feel guilty and make us feel that we are turning against God because we give up our old religious beliefs that we have now been informed are false.

The rich young man who came to Jesus had trouble giving up his attachment to outer things. Jesus suggested that he sell all he had and give it away. Jesus was not opposed to having things but he wanted to make his point with the young man that following inner guidance is more important than the things. If the young man had been willing to do what Jesus suggested he would have discovered that he could have had the best of both worlds, the inner and the outer.

Another man came to Jesus one time and wanted to follow Him and be a disciple. He probably said something like this to Jesus, "Jesus, I like what you have to say and I want to go along with you but let me first bury my father." Jesus said to him, "Let the dead bury the dead." Jesus was not hard hearted and cruel in making this statement. He was only stressing the important point that seeking the truth is more important than all human relationships, all traditions, and all human rules and regulations that we might think are so important. We get so enamoured and in love with our outer human views about life and our human relationships that we want to nourish them, and keep them alive.

The greatest honor we can give to both outer, human parents and our inner parents is to make a commitment to seek the truth and to follow it when it is discovered. The outer human parents may not see this as honor or respect but they are blind. They may even think of us as rebellious and disrespectful but we cannot control their attitudes and the way they interpret what we are doing. We do not have to become obnoxious in our search for truth but we cannot let anyone, any human relationship keep us from our search.

The inner parents may also feel rejected and neglected. We get used to thinking in human terms and we are reluctant to change and follow the inner guidance wholeheartedly and sincerely. But that is just what we have to do. It is the only way to true happiness and it is the only way to true spiritual growth.

To honor our parents is not to do everything they tell us to do. We can love them and be true to our inner self. We can know that some day they too will come to know their oneness with their own inner Lord. If we are not true to this inner Higher Self we will be miserable and unhappy. It may be a humanly painful experience to be rejected by those we love but we will find that what Jesus said is true. He expressed this pain in the analogy of a woman giving birth to a child. He said that while she was in travail she would be in much pain. But when the child was born she would forget about the pain and her heart and mind would be filled with great joy over the new child. It may be painful when truth is born in our consciousness. But if we will be patient and meet the possible human rejection with love we will discover the joy Jesus referred to, the joy of knowing the truth about our relationship with God, the joy of knowing that we are truly sons and daughters of the one true God. And this joy no human being can take away from us.

The Sixth Commandment

Thou Shalt Not Kill.

De. 5:17

This commandment causes much confusion, for when we read the Old Testament we find many stories that tell of killing. You will recall that the penalty for breaking some of these commandments is death. When Joshua was told by God to take the city of Jericho, he was told to kill everyone, even children.

It would seem from all this killing that the Hebrews had little regard for human life. But this is not the case. They held human life very dear and sacred. The very first chapter of Genesis tells us that man is created in the image and likeness of God. That is a very high form of idealism.

The sixth commandment was actually given for the preservation of life. It was for the protection of the individual. They did not have a court system as we have today and when someone was killed it was left to the next of kin to seek out the offending party and put him to death. The commandment was especially given for the protection of those who were members of the Covenant Community and it probably should read, "You shall not murder" rather than kill.

Many have used this commandment as a basis for vegetarianism. But it did not have this meaning for the ones for whom it was given. The Hebrews were not vegetarians. Jesus was a Jew and He ate meat. The last supper consisted of lamb. And one morning when Jesus appeared to the disciples after

the resurrection He had prepared a breakfast for them consist-
ing of fish. The killing of animals was performed regularly in
the Temple as part of the sacrificial system. So this commandment cannot be used to justify the practice of vegetarianism. If
one wants to be a vegetarian and is guided to do so by his or
her own indwelling Spirit then they should be vegetarian. And
if they are being guided in this way they do not need some
outer Biblical justification for the practice. The inner guidance
is enough.

The commandment was not meant to apply to capital
punishment. As I have already said, even members of the
community were killed if they violated any of the commandments of God that required severe punishment. We should
keep in mind that for these poeple severe punishment acted as
a deterrent in many instances and the carrying out of the death
sentence was a public display. Some have used this commandment as a basis for their reasoning against killing in wars. But
here again the Hebrews did not think that way. They were told
many times by God to go into battle and much killing of
barbarians and pagans took place.

I am pointing out these facts, not because I believe in
killing in war and in capital punishment but simply to help
solve the problem of confusion that many have about this
commandment. I personally feel that capital punishment does
not solve the problem that those who believe in it think it will
solve. Just removing someone from society does not solve the
problem. If you can accept it, it only causes the same problem
over agian when that individual soul reincarnates again in
another body. It is quite ironic that in our Christian teaching
we think that death is necessary in order to go to heaven. And
we also think that death is a form of punishment for criminals.
Paul thought of death as punishment. He said, "The wages of
sin is death." So you can see we are not quite consistent or
logical in our thought about life or death.

There is a religious meaning to this commandment that
we moderns do not understand, but it was a very powerful
thing for the Hebrews. It was the idea that the spilling of blood

polluted not only the family of the deceased but also the nation of Israel. It was the religious obligation for the next of kin to seek out the offender and kill that person. Whenever blood was spilled they believed that the family and nation were both contaminated. Murder was a crime against the family and the bloodguilt had to be purged and purified from the family and nation. Remember, they did not have a court system and it was up to the murdered person's family to carry out the retribution.

It was not simply to punish the offender, it was for purifying and cleansing that the offender had to be killed. The family member who carried out the killing in order that justice could take place was called the "avenger." He was also called "redeemer." The dead man's family and also the country of Israel was under the deceased's wrath until justice was carried out and the offender was put to death. In Judges 8:21 we are told the story in which Gideon killed two men, Zebah and Zalmunna, because they killed his brother. It was Gideon's obligation to do this. And in II Samuel 3:27 we are told another story in which Joab, the commander-in-chief in David's army, killed a man named Abner because Abner had killed Joab's brother, Asahel.

These people believed that only vengeance could dissolve or purify and absolve the bloodguilt on the family and nation. Even an animal that killed a human had to be put to death. Moses expressed this vengeance or compensation in this way: "And if any mischief follow, then thou shalt give life for life, eye for eye, tooth for tooth, hand for hand, foot for foot." (Ex. 21:23-24) It is further stated in verse 25: "Burning for burning and stripe for stripe." All bloodshed brought guilt, even the killing in self-defense and by accident, and even this shedding of blood had to be purified. We are told in the Bible that God required this retribution. God speaking to Noah said, "Whoso sheddeth man's blood, by man shall his blood be shed: for in the image of God made he man." (Gen. 9:6)

In the case of accidental killing, the individual responsible could take refuge in one of six cities in Israel that had been designated for this purpose. When Joshua divided up the land amongst the twelve tribes, eleven of them got territory and one of them, the Levites, were designated as the priests and were among all the tribes. The six cities were known as the "cities of refuge." The individual who thought he had killed by accident could go to one of these cities and the family avenger could not kill him there. It was here that the individual could have his case brought before the citizens to determine whether he had committed murder or whether the killing was an accident. They had three basic principles by which they judged intent. The first was called "laying in wait." If the offender was actually hiding and waiting for an opportunity to kill the deceased, then it was considered murder. If it was known that the two individuals were angry with each other and fussed and argued and fought at times then this would be evidence that murder had taken place and the killing was not an accident. The third principle was whether or not the individual used some implement that was ordinarily used for killing; if so, it was not an accident. It would be considered that he intended to kill and would be pronounced guilty. However, if the individual was found innocent then he would be free to return to his home and the avenger or redeemer could not kill him. These principles for determination of guilt or innocence are given in Numbers, chapter 35.

The idea that blood pollutes the land is told in Numbers 35:33 and it reads, "So ye shall not pollute the land wherein ye are: for blood it defileth the land: and the land cannot be cleansed of the blood that is shed therein, but by the blood of him that shed it." It is quite ironic that blood was being constantly shed in the Temple worship but this was different in their thinking. It just goes to show that religious beliefs and practices are not always logical.

If an individual was found guilty in one of the cities of refuge he would be taken outside the city and stoned. The witnesses would put their hands on his head, for they believed that the guilt upon the family and the nation would be transferred to the accused person. The witnesses would then

cast the first stone and then the people of the community who
were present would also cast stones on the accused until he
was dead. This reminds us of the story about Jesus and the
woman accused of adultery. Jesus said that the one without sin
should cast the first stone. The practice or belief that guilt can
be transferred was also picked up by the Christians. Jesus took
upon himself the sins and guilt of humanity and His death
brought about the possibility of purification. It was believed
and still is to this day that every child born into this world is
guilty of sin, original sin, and that it has to be redeemed. Jesus
is the redeemer. It came to be accepted that only an innocent
one could take on the guilt of the sinner and atone for him.
During the time when the Temple was in full operation,
animals were used in sacrifice. The blood of the innocent
animal was sprinkled upon the altar and upon other things as a
way of purifying and atoning for the guilt of the sinner. This
atonement would reestablish the innocence of the sinner. To
be innocent was to be just or in a right and true relationship
with God. Sin broke that relationship. Paul referred to this
reestablishment of a proper and true relationship with God as
"justification by faith."

What is the deeper and even more beneficial spiritual
teaching in this commandment? Outer killing does not just
happen. It is caused by something that begins in the consciousness of an individual. It begins when a person may take
offense regarding someone's actions or what another might say
that is considered as an insult. It begins within an individual as
anger, hate, and a desire for revenge. Jesus brought this out
when He said, "Ye have heard that it was said by them of old
time, Thou shalt not kill; and whosoever shall kill shall be in
danger of the judgment." (Mat. 5:21) The judgment is not
referring to some day in the future when all the world will be
judged. Jesus is saying that killing would disrupt the relationship that the individual has with God. In other words the
individual would be out of harmony with the divine. He goes
on to say, "But I say unto you, That whosoever is angry with
his brother without a cause shall be in danger of the judgment."

Not only the act of killing but even the inner desire to kill will disturb the inner relationship that the individual may have with God. Jesus further states, "And whosoever shall say to his brother, Raca, shall be in danger of the council." Raca was a word meaning some form of abuse that is less than killing or murder, and Jesus was saying that they could come under condemnation by some council. You will recall Jesus was hauled before a council and was beaten. The same happened to Paul a number of times. Continuing on, Jesus says, "But whosoever shall say, Thou fool, shall be in danger of hell fire." (Mat. 5:21-22) This has been interpreted to mean that some day the person would go to a place referred to as hell and suffer for eternity. But there is no such place. The hell is a description of the inner torment, frustration, despair, and anguish that a person experiences when he thinks of another person in a negative way. It is the old attitude expressed in the statement, "You make me sick." It is not the other person that is making the individual ill with his behaviour; it is the attitudes and emotions held in consciousness that are causing the inner torment.

The phrase "without cause" was probably an interpolation and was inserted by someone who wanted to have an excuse for continuing to hate and for justification of revenge. Jesus probably did not say this, for He knew that anger would disturb the sensitive balance of harmony of the soul and there were no exceptions. A person may feel that he has good reason to be angry but in principle there is no good reason. All anger will disturb the inner tranquility of the soul and revenge will not satisfy or dissolve it. Hate can never bring about justification, the reestablishment of a right and true relationship with God. Only agape love can do that. Agape love is unconditional love. It is the love that God has for all of us. His love is given freely and there are no prerequisites for receiving it. It is given to guilty individuals as well as to the innocent ones. The only thing is that violations of principle will keep us from realizing and experiencing His love. That is why forgiveness is necessary in every instance and there are no exceptions. No one can express that love for us; we have to be open and receptive channels for its free and unconditional expression through us.

Judgment is all the negative consequences that come about in our lives, either as some outer event or as some health problem. However, we must be careful and not think that all health challenges or problems that we encounter are due to negative causes in consciousness. Sometimes the reestablishment of a right relationship with God can cause what we think of as negative results but are really not that at all. Positive and constructive thought and feeling can bring as severe or even more severe outer results. For example when we begin to exercise certain muscles they will get sore. Stepping out in faith may cause financial loss. An individual may pray for prosperity and lose his job or business and this may be a necessary preparation for something better. It may be that he would never give up his job or business voluntarily and he may need this jolt to prod him on to greater heights and greater blessings. The human ego is very cautious when it comes to security. It always wants to be sure of success and have guarantees before it steps out in faith.

Getting back into a right relationship with God in our thinking and expectations may also cause the pain of severing cherished relationships. It may require of us that we give up certain desires and the expectations of success along personal lines that would be out of harmony with our true purpose or the divine plan for our lives.

The truth student who is always looking for the easy, quick, no effort, overnight way to success and prosperity will probably never find it. He or she will keep looking for the teacher who is going to reveal the hidden "secret" that will take all the pain and effort out of getting rich, the teacher who will tell him or her how to get money, success, fame, and many other goodies without the necessity of changing consciousness. Many will spend their whole lives in this fruitless search simply because they are unwilling to accept the challenge of spiritual growth. Spiritual growth can be painful, but it can also be joyful. The refusal to accept the challenge of spiritual growth will be more painful, for it will lead to a life of inner and outer frustration, despair, and failure. I say this, not because I am a pessimist, but I say it to help dissolve some misconceptions and false illusions that many have about the study of truth. New ideas coming into consciousness can be very disturbing. Jesus pointed this out when He said, "I have yet may things to say unto you, but ye cannot bear them now." (John 16:12) His disciples were having a very difficult time grasping, understanding, and accepting what He was trying to teach them. He told them they would meet with opposition from their family and friends and they would also experience inner frustration, fear, doubt, and apprehension. But He said if they would only stand firm they would come to realize an inner peace and joy that they had never known before. His joy would be made full in them.

When new ideas of truth come to us we should not kill them with our rejection. We should not call them crazy, stupid, foolish, or designate them as being negative and impractical. We should not kill another's joy and enthusiasm by condemning his or her ideas that they may share with us. Even if we think the ideas are impractical we should not kill them. We should let others have the freedom to enjoy their own spiritual growth. We should be especially careful that we do not label our negative criticism as being helpful. What may seem impractical to us may be very practical to another person. We can also kill by listening to and believing in negative rumors about others. We may kill the good opinion we had about another person. Instead of seeing the person as a child of God we see him as a "fool" just because we listened to someone's negative assessment. Jesus cautioned us about this. The way we perceive others, the way we think and feel about them, will have a very decided negative effect upon us and we therefore should avoid this negation.

We should also be careful and not kill our own good thoughts, feelings, and ideas about ourselves. Self-criticism leads to self-destruction. It leads to failure and many other unpleasant consequences.

What is the solution? The only one is to let God's unconditional love express through us. This will take faith and courage but it is the only way. We have tried to bring about peace in the world by killing those who are different in thought, personality, religion, and race. But peace will never be established that way. Wars do not solve anything; they only prepare for more warfare. Only love can bring peace, contentment, happiness, health, prosperity for all people. The sooner we get around to the business of letting God's unconditional love express through us the sooner we will have our individual inner peace and security and we will be making a great contribution toward the elimination of both inner and outer killing. We will be contributing to eternal life, joy, peace, and happiness for all.

The Seventh Commandment

Neither Shalt Thou
Commit Adultery.

De. 5:18

This particular commandment has been the cause of much frustration and guilt for many people over the years. It has been used by the church to make people feel they were living in sin and out of favor with God. Even today many are living miserable lives because they interpret this commandment rather literally. They continue to live in a marriage relationship because they believe that if they get a divorce and remarry that they will be living in sin or adultery. However, you will note that this commandment does not say anything about divorce being adultery; it only says one should not commit adultery. The divorce aspect is attributed to Jesus and that is a highly questionable subject which we will consider as we continue our openminded look into a better understanding of why this commandment was given to the Hebrews many years ago.

First of all we must ask the question, "What is adultery?" For the Hebrews, for whom the commandment was given, it was this. If a man, married or single, had sexual relations with a married woman, both were guilty of committing adultery. If a man had sexual relations with a single woman, then it was considered to be fornication and this was not as serious as adultery. However, if a single woman got involved with a man before she was married it could lead to very serious consequences later. If, when she did get married, her husband discovered that she was not a virgin, he could have her brought before the elders for trial. If she was found guilty she could then be stoned to death. The penalty for adultery is recorded in Deuteronomy 22:22 and it reads, "If a man be found lying with a woman married to an husband, then they shall both of them die, both the man that lay with the woman, and the woman: so shalt thou put away evil from Israel."

This penalty applied not only to a married woman but it also applied to a betrothed woman, one that we would consider today as being engaged. Two witnesses were needed in order to prove the woman guilty of adultery. If the husband did not have the witnesses but was suspicious that his wife was having an affair, as we would say today, then he could have her tried under what was called the "water of jealousy." This was a rather sordid ordeal for the woman to go through and probably many admitted their guilt rather than go through it. If you want to read about this ordeal or trial you may do so. It is recorded in Number 5:11-31. It is no doubt based upon the psychology that if a person is guilty they will get a negative reaction from drinking the bitter water prepared by the priest. We would call this today a psychosomatic reaction.

Why did they have such stern and severe punishment for the violation of this commandment? For one thing you will recall that these primitive peoples believed that they continued their existence through their children. It was very important to them that they have a male child in order that they might continue to live. Therefore, the husband wanted to be sure that any children his wife had were his own. Another reason was that adultery was a violation of the property rights of the male. The woman was considered his personal property and he was very jealous of these rights. This jealousy is revealed in the passage in Numbers that I have referred to. For any man to violate the rights of another male was serious and quite often deadly business. A man could have affairs with unmarried women if they were willing to take the risk but as has been mentioned she could be prosecuted later when it was discovered that she was not a virgin. A husband could have affairs with other women in his household, namely his concubines or slaves. A concubine was a Hebrew female that had been purchased from some poor father who might be in need of some ready cash. Females were not considered to be very valuable in these primitive times. Many would be exposed to die when they were born. A concubine was a Hebrew slave but many households had foreign women who were also slaves serving the family. A wife could not do anything about these affairs that her husband may have with these other women. In fact, sometimes the wife recommended that her husband have relations with a concubine. If she was unfortunate in not having children she would make this recommendation as Sarah did to Abraham when she was up in years and thought she would never have any children. It was just as important to the wife to have a male child as it was for the husband.

You will recall from your study of the life of Jacob that he also had relations with his wife's handmaidens, Zilpah and Bilhah. After Jacob fled from his brother Esau he went to the land where his mother's brother Laban lived and fell in love with Rachel. He agreed to work seven years for Laban so that he could marry his daughter. However, he had a great surprise when he discovered that the woman he got on his wedding night in the tent was not Rachel but her sister, Leah. When he rebuked his father-in-law about this, Laban reminded him that the older daughter had to marry first. But Laban agreed to let Jacob have Rachel if he would agree to work for him another seven years. Because of his great love for Rachel, Jacob agreed to do this. He did have one consolation and it was this. He could have Rachel as his wife right away and then work for seven years as payment for her. The first time he had to work seven years before he was supposed to get her and got Leah instead. Out of the marriages of Leah and Rachel and their two handmaidens Jacob had the twelve sons that eventually became the heads of the twelve tribes of Israel. In our modern day thinking we would say this is adultery and think of it as very evil for a man to have several wives and to have sexual relations with the maids in the household. But for these primitive peoples it was something very religious.

When we understand the Hebrew concept we can see that Joseph was probably very shocked when he found out that Mary was expecting a child and he knew he was not the father. We are so used to this story that we do not realize the serious trouble Mary was in. However, at that time she could not be put to death, for the Jews were living under Roman law which prohibited them from executing capital punishment without the permission of the Roman governor. In the story that tells of the adulterous woman that was brought to Jesus we know the woman would not have been stoned for it would have been a violation of Roman law and the Jews would have been in serious trouble for taking the law into their own hands. The story is told in order to put Jesus on the spot. Which law would he violate? Would he go against Rome? Jewish law said that a woman guilty of adultery had to be stoned. Jesus gave a very neat answer. He said, "He that is without sin among you, let him first cast a stone at her." (John 8:7)

In the Sermon on the Mount we have some passages that have been quite challenging for many people. In Matthew 5:27-28 we read, "Ye have heard that it was said by them of old time, Thou shalt not commit adultery: But I say unto you, That whosoever looketh on a woman to lust after her hath committed adultery with her already in his heart." The point Jesus is making in this statement is that outer acts that are not right and beneficial have their beginning in the mind and heart, the thought and feeling of the individual. This applies not only to sex but it applies to everything. In this instance Jesus is teaching the importance for the individual to control his or her passions. If one learns to discipline himself he can avoid getting involved in relations and situations that may only cause him much misery and many problems.

In Matthew 19:6 we have another statement that is attributed to Jesus that has been the cause of much guilt on the part of individuals who have divorced their mates. The statement reads, "What therefore God hath joined together, let not man put asunder." This has been used as a scriptural basis for the prohibition against divorce. But let us ask the question, "How does God join two people together?" Is God some personal Being that intervenes in the lives of people, saying they have to marry certain individuals? I doubt this is the case. Are two people joined together by God simply because they stand in front of a minister, priest, rabbi or a justice of the peace and say, "I do"? Many couples do this but are they being joined together by God? The answer in many instances is no. It was the practice in ancient times for the parents to make the arrangements for their daughter's wedding. People get married for many other reasons even today. Some get married for money, fame, security, escape from unbearable family relationships, and for any number of reasons. We cannot say that just because they say "I do" and sign some legal documents required by the state that God has joined them together. Some people get married because of powerful and uncontrolled passions.

It is not the outer ceremony that binds people together. God is love and a true marriage takes place when love binds people together. It is especially important to realize that I am saying "love." There is a great deal of difference between love and passion and many have not learned to recognize this difference. Many think they are the same thing. Divorce was only one of many problems the early Church had to deal with. Many early Christians were Jews and no doubt many were from the liberal Hillel school of thought that permitted divorce for almost any reason. The Shammai school was more conservative. One way to deal with this problem would be to put the prohibitions against divorce in the mouth of Jesus. I doubt seriously whether Jesus would advise two people to remain together if passion was their only reason for being together. Jesus would know that this was not a relationship that was brought about by God. If a couple have made a mistake and have married in the heat of passion and there is no love involved in their relationship then it is not wrong for them to dissolve it. In fact it might be the best thing they could do, especially if children are involved. The old belief that they should stay together for the sake of the children is negative and the results could be damaging not only to the parents but also the children. Children can sense the underlying bitterness and lack of love between two parents who do not love each other.

When we consider the writings of Paul we find that he was not against divorce and his writings were in circulation in many Christian churches before any of the Gospels were written. For example in I Cor. 7:12-16 Paul says, "But to the rest speak I, not the Lord: If any brother hath a wife that believeth not, and she be pleased to dwell with him, let him not put her away. And the woman which hath an husband that believeth not, and if he be pleased to dwell with her, let her not leave him. For the unbelieving husband is sanctified by the wife, and the unbelieving wife is sanctified by the husband: else were your children unclean; but now are they holy. But if the unbelieving depart, let him depart. A brother or sister is not under bondage in such cases: but God hath called us to peace. For what knowest thou, O wife, whether thou shalt save thy husband? or how knowest thou, O man, whether thou shalt save thy wife?" This passage is the basis for the permitting of divorce in the Catholic Church in certain instances and is called the "Pauline privilege." The Gospel of Matthew makes written many years after this Corinthian letter by Paul, probably at least 25 or maybe 30 years later. Matthew makes Jesus very conservative. According to him Jesus is supposed to have said, "And I say unto you, Whosoever shall put away his wife, except it be for fornication, and shall marry another, committeth adultery; and whoso marrieth her which is put away doth commit adultery." (Mat. 19:9) It is believed by traditional Biblical scholars that the phrase, "except for fornication" is a later addition. In all probability the whole statement is put into the mouth of Jesus in order to strengthen the authority of the church over the life of the individual. There are other passages in the Bible that have been attributed to Jesus that He probably did not say. This may seem like a heretical statement but it is the view of many traditional Biblical scholars and not just my opinion.

How can we make practical sense out of all the confusion and guilt that this commandment causes in people today? In order to answer this question we must first ask another question and it is this: "What is the purpose of sex?" Sex is a biological process and its main purpose is to give disembodied souls another opportunity to reenter a physical body so that those souls may continue their journey toward a full conscious realization of oneness with God. It gives the soul another opportunity to mature spiritually, another opportunity to achieve the ultimate objective in life, another opportunity to become free through a knowledge of the Truth. It is another opportunity for the soul to rebuild the body temple and eventually overcome the last enemy that Paul referred to as physical death. Jesus also said the same thing. If a person entered the kingdom of God, the consciousness of the inner Presence of God, he would experience eternal life and would not come into condemnation but would pass from death into life.

This is no doubt one of those "hard sayings" of Jesus and it gets even harder when we read the rest of it. Jesus continues to say, "All men cannot receive this saying, save they to whom it is given. For there are some eunuchs, which were so born from their mother's womb; and there are some eunuchs, which were made eunuchs of men; and there be eunuchs, which have made themselves eunuchs for the kingdom of heaven's sake. He that is able to receive it, let him receive it." (Mat. 19:11-12) And you know the rest of the story where Jesus said that there is no marriage in the kingdom of heaven. Origen, one of the great teachers in the early church, literally castrated himself because of this statement, thinking it would help him overcome all sexual temptations and make it possible for him to enter the kingdom of heaven. But it did not work for him and that is not the way into the kingdom. The way into the kingdom is through a total receptivity to God's love and this means that one must learn to control his physical passions and appetites and not try to eliminate them.

When love is involved in a relationship between two individuals there is no desire to have just a casual, passionate experience with another person. When love is involved the individuals are willing to accept the responsibility of their actions. When love is involved the individuals can be trusted in their relationship. When love is involved both parties will exercise self-control over the passions. When love is involved there will be respect for the relationship. When love is involved there will be no desire to adulterate the relationship with extracurricular affairs. I suppose I should say, when love is involved and one has learned to discipline his passions, then he or she will not get involved in relationships that will only lead to problems. If one does not have that self-discipline and does get involved, he or she will experience guilt. When this happens the couple will have to evaluate their relationship and determine whether it is based on love or passion. If it is based on passion they may decide to end the relationship. If it is based on love and it can be reconciled through forgiveness then they may decide to continue the relationship.

The concept of adultery is a social-religious term used to control the behavior and actions of individuals. It is not the expression of a principle. Principle never changes. Marriage customs and laws change constantly. What is considered wrong or adulterous today was very permissible and even considered religious in Biblical times. King Solomon had 700 wives and 300 concubines. It was right for him and he could afford it. It would be wrong for anyone today even if they could afford such a harem. Monogamy did not come into the Hebrew lifestyle until after the Babylonian Captivity. When we learn to reason in the light of eternal, unchanging principle, then if multiple relationships were not wrong for Abraham, Jacob, and Solomon and others, they should not be wrong today. That is, if they were based upon eternal, unchanging principles. However, this is not justification for having multiple affairs today. For that can lead to serious, negative consequences.

The allegorical method of interpreting scripture can be even more helpful to us today regarding this commandment. This method of interpreting has nothing to do with outer sexual relationships. In consciousness the male represents intellectual thoughts and the female represents the feeling nature. So what it is saying to us is that we should not commit adultery by uniting a negative feeling and a positive and constructive thought; or just the opposite. Do not divorce or give up a combination of thought and feeling which is right, true, and good. Have you ever felt that you should do something but reasoned or rationalized your way out of it? Have you ever had a good thought and felt it was impractical or felt incapable and therefore did not get married in thought and feeling in order that the good thought or idea could be expressed? That is metaphysical adultery. Do not adulterate intuitive spiritual guidance for any reason.

If one will listen to the still small voice of Spirit, he or she will learn to exercise control over the passions. When this happens the individual will not get involved in any relationship that will cause problems. He or she will realize that excessive and indiscriminate expression and indulgence in passions is a biologically depleting experience. He or she will also realize that overindulgence or excessive sexual activity leads to mental, emotional and even physical complications and problems. It leads to a loss of vitality and energy. Even if a couple is married, overindulgence can be very depleting of the mental and physical energy. It can also diminish the creative capacity of the mind.

We should always endeavor to strike a harmonious balance and keep the passions on a high level. When we do so then there will be a harmony and peace in mind and health in the body temple.

The Eighth Commandment

Neither Shalt Thou Steal.

De. 5:18

Today we think of stealing as taking something that belongs to another. We think of it as robbing a person or a business or a home. However, at the time this commandment was given, it was a more serious problem and it covered more than we usually associate with it. Whenever a law is formulated to prohibit something it must be that it is covering something that is prevalent in that society.

I suppose the most serious stealing that was taking place not only in the Hebrew society but in all ancient societies was the kidnapping of someone and selling him or her as a slave. In the story of Joseph in the Old Testament you will recall that his brothers sold him to a caravan of traders on their way to Egypt and that he was sold in Egypt to a man named Potiphar. Joseph refers to this experience in Genesis 40:15. There he says, "For indeed I was stolen away out of the land of the Hebrews: and here also have I done nothing that they should put me into the dungeon." At the time he made this statement he was in prison. He had rejected the advances of Potiphar's wife. She got angry at him and told her husband that Joseph had made advances to her and Joseph wound up in prison.

In De. 24:7 we are told that this type of stealing is a capital offense and that the thief, if caught, could be put to death. The passage reads, "If a man be found stealing any of his brethren of the children of Israel, and maketh merchandise of him, or selleth him; then that thief shall die; and thou shalt put evil away from among you." It was important in their thinking because the whole nation could suffer the displeasure of Yahweh and that could be quite devastating. Take for example the story of Joshua and his invasion of the land of Canaan. When Joshua captured the city of Jericho he was told by God that he was not to take anything from the city and that every living thing must be destroyed. All men, women, and children were to be killed. The city was under the "ban," which was the curse of God. However, one individual could not resist temptation. The Hebrews, just coming out of 40 years wandering in a desert wilderness, probably saw the riches of the city of Jericho as a great temptation. Well, this man, named Achan, took some clothing and gold and silver from the city. He thought he could get away with this. Joshua, thinking how easy it was to take Jericho, thought it would be just as easy to take the next city, Ai. He sent a force of 3,000 men to take the city but they were soundly defeated. This was discouraging to Joshua for he believed that God would make them successful. When he sought the reason for the defeat he was told that someone had violated the "ban" on Jericho and that was why they were defeated at Ai. Joshua was told to find the culprit and put him to death. Achan was found out to be the culprit and he and his family were killed. Joshua then attacked the city of Ai again and was successful and victorious. The nation was affected because of the sin of one man. When the nation was purified by the elimination of that man and his family then they were blessed with success.

In Exodus 21:16 we read, "And he that stealeth a man, and selleth him, or if he be found in his hand, he shall surely be put to death." You will note in this passage it does not say a Hebrew, so the implication is any man. The law also applied to wages. In Lev. 19:13 we read, "Thou shalt not defraud thy neighbor, neither rob him: the wages of him that is hired shall not abide with thee all night until the morning." In other words the employer is not to try and cheat the individual out of his wages for any reason. Neither is the employer to take advantage of a man simply because he is poor. The law states, "Thou shalt not oppress an hired servant that is poor and needy . . ." De. 24:14.

Taking someone's property without that person's consent was considered stealing. It was also a violation of this commandment if one was careless with another's property when he had the consent of the owner. One must treat another's property as if it were his own. If a person borrowed an animal and the animal was injured or killed while in his possession, he would have to make restitution. If he could not make restitution, which could be anywhere from twice the value up to as much as five times the value, then he could be sold as a slave. An ox would be of more value than a sheep, for if the ox was put out of commission it could have a very detrimental effect upon the owner's livelihood. If the offender was sold as a slave the money from the sale would go to the injured party. This is quite different in our society. In our society if a person injures someone and at the same time has violated a state or city law and the state or city fines him for that violation, the state keeps the money. The injured party gets nothing. This does not seem quite fair since the state was not injured. But it is like Plato said, where there are laws there is bound to be injustice.

There was a peculiar thing related to this law. If a burglar was killed while robbing a house and it happened at night time, then the homicide would be considered justified. However, if the robbery took place in the daytime, the one being robbed could not kill the burglar. If he was fortunate enough to catch him he could sell him as a slave and restitution could be made in this way.

We have an old saying in our culture which states, "Finders keepers, losers weepers." This would not be acceptable under this commandment. If a man's property is found, an animal or any inanimate object, the person finding the property must make an all-out effort to find the owner and return the property. He had to do this whether he liked the owner or not. He could not, like some today, say that it is his simply because he found it and did not know who it belonged to.

To make this commandment more relevant for us today there are a number of questions we might ask. For example, "Is stealing ever justified?" Some would say yes. Their reasoning would be that if a person is hungry it is OK to steal in order to get food if he has no money to buy it. However, that is not logical reasoning. Instead of stealing, why not ask the person who seems to have more than enough to help him? Many steal in order to buy drugs that they do not need. They get hooked on some drug and then have to rob and steal in order to pay for the drugs to sustain their habit. Some rationalize theft by saying the person from whom they take something has more than he needs. But this makes no difference. It does not matter how much wealth another person has; we have no right to take it. This applies to corporations and companies and it applies to nations who are trying to enforce a communistic type of society by spreading the wealth of the nation around.

Another and even more important question that leads to some very challenging thought is, "Why is stealing considered wrong?" Stealing is wrong because it is a violation of principle and every violation of principle has its negative consequences. Stealing is a violation of the principle of love. Stealing is a violation of the principle of compensation, the law of cause and effect. The thief thinks that if he can outwit the cops or the owner of some property that he can get away with his crime. But the truth is he can never get away with it. Oh, it may seem for a time that he is getting away with it. He may even laugh about his crime and take great pride in the fact that he was smart enough to pull off the big one. But sometime, somewhere along the eternal pathway of life there will have to be a divine reckoning. Paul brings this out very clearly in his letter to the church at Galatia. He tells them, "Be not deceived; God is not mocked; for whatsoever a man soweth, that shall he also reap." (Gal. 6:7)

Now here is the big challenge in our thought that may be of help to us in understanding this principle. The reaping may not always be in the lifetime in which the crime or theft takes place. This is why it seems that many are sowing or stealing or doing other negative things and seemingly are getting away with it. But as Paul tells us, we should not be deceived by this apparent contradiction. If you would like to make a more detailed study of this principle you might want to read the book *Many Mansions* by Gina Cerminara. This book is based on the readings of Edgar Cayce. Many people came to Cayce for help in healing. In many instances the information revealed through Cayce in his trance state contained not only instructions that would help bring about the healing but quite often the individual would be told what he did in a previous lifetime that caused the illness or whatever other problem the person was experiencing in this lifetime. In other words the individual was reaping the consequences of actions that he might have thought he got away with in another lifetime.

It is said that the wheels of justice grind slowly but they do grind. Many are deceived because they do not understand the principle of cause and effect or sowing and reaping. It is stressed throughout the Old Testament. Jesus stressed it in the analogy of the good tree bringing forth good fruit and the evil tree bringing forth evil fruit. Jesus stressed the principle in the Golden Rule. Why should we do to others as we want them to do to us? The answer is simple. As we do to others it will be done to us. It may not be done by the one to whom we do something but some negative reaction will come our way. Lest we think the principle only works in a negative way we should remember that it works even better in a positive and constructive way.

Jesus stressed the positive application of the principle when he said, "Give and it shall be given unto you, good measure, pressed down, shaken together and running over." The Mosaic law stressed the principle from the negative point when it stated an eye for an eye and tooth for a tooth. In physics the principle is stated, "For every action there is an opposite and equal reaction.

This is a universal principle that we are dealing with and it goes far beyond Judaism. The principle applies to everyone, regardless of his or her religious beliefs. It applies to Christians,

Buddhists, Hindus, and Moslems. It applies to those who do not have any religious affiliation or any religious faith. It applies to the atheists as well. It applies to the rich and the poor. It applies to the wise and the unwise. It applies to the adult and the infant. It makes no difference whether the infant knows better or not. If an infant puts his hand on a hot stove he will be burned just as much and as fast as an adult will. We are living in a just universe. It would not be just if the laws of life played favorites. It would not be just if a person could do evil and reap good benefits. It may seem that he is able to do this for a while but sooner or later the principle of compensation will bring about what we refer to as judgment. Judgment is the day when restitution must be made and the purifying process begins to take place to restore balance in the life and soul of the individual who is in violation of principle.

Another way of thinking about stealing is the attempt that many people make in trying to get something for nothing. That is an impossibility. It is considered stealing when we do not give our best to the person or company that we agree to work for. It is stealing when one tries to get customers from another by criticizing or giving false information about his competitor. There is stealing such as this that takes place even in the Christian church. This form of stealing is referred to as "sheep stealing." Some ministers are very competitive and want everyone to attend their churches. There is stealing that takes place in corporations. One company may try to steal the talented individuals working for another company. The stealing of ideas and inventions is constantly going on. That is why we have patent and copyright laws. The Russians seek to steal scientific knowledge from the U.S. I do not know if we try to steal from the Russians but we probably do. This same type of interchange of theft may even be going on between the U.S. and Japan. There are many subtle ways that theft takes place.

When love is active in consciousness we lose all human desire to try and get something unjustly or through devious means and methods. In fact we are transformed to the extent that we understand what Jesus meant when He said, "Give and you shall receive." We discover that there is such a rich potential of ideas within us that we do not have to steal from others. We do not have to steal their ideas and we do not have to steal their possessions. All we have to do is tune in to our own creative potential and we will have more than enough of everything to take care of all our desires and physical needs. We will not have to try and get an advantage over someone else. We will find that it is much more of a blessing to give advantages than to try and get them.

What should be our attitude when something is stolen from us? It should not be one of hate and resentment. And it should not be a feeling of loss. We should realize and know that what is stolen can be replaced. What is rightfully ours will always be brought back into our experience. Either the thing stolen or its equivalent will be returned. Knowing this we can find peace of mind. We can always be assured that God will provide for all our needs. No thief can take that assurance from us. Jesus stated this when He said, "Store up for yourself treasures in heaven where thieves do not break through and steal." When we have this consciousness of oneness with God, thieves cannot take that from us.

If a person is unduly upset over some loss by theft it may be there is a need to let go of overattachment to material things. There may be a need to consider if too much emphasis is placed on having something, thinking it is the source of happiness. We must constantly remind ourselves that God is the Source of all that we need. When we are in tune with the Source, things are provided and thieves cannot have power over us. Faith in the inner Source is our security and our outer prosperity.

The Ninth Commandment

Neither Shalt Thou Bear False Witness Against Thy Neighbor.

De. 5:20

Two witnesses were required for conviction for any crime. In De. 17:6 we read, "At the mouth of two witnesses, or three witnesses, shall he that is worthy of death be put to death; but at the mouth of one witness he shall not be put to death." Just think, two people could testify against someone and that person could be put to death or convicted of any type of crime. I suppose that is why there were severe penalties for giving false testimony.

The reliability of a witness was determined by his character and his past life. Women and slaves were not permitted to witness, only males. This may seem that the Hebrews had a low opinion of women. But in fact they did not. They had a high regard for women. A woman was considered personal property and she was vital for the continuation of life and what they thought of as personal existence. Witnesses did not take an oath; they were expected to tell the truth. If a witness gave false testimony and was found out he would have to suffer the consequences of what he was accusing the other person. If he was witnessing falsely that someone had committed murder, he could be put to death himself.

False testimony could be very damaging to a person. A man's status in the community could be ruined. His very life could be at stake, especially if two people got together to plot against him. A person who witnessed a serious crime was obligated to bring about prosecution. When a verdict of guilty was handed down, the usual method for punishing a capital offense was by stoning. In more serious crimes even more severe and torturous methods were used, such as burning in a fire. The witnesses would cast the first stones, then the people would follow in like manner until the victim was dead.

When Paul survived a stoning it was probably due to the fact that the people at that time were breaking Roman law. This is an indication of how much they hated Paul and what he was saying that they would risk breaking Roman law, for the Romans were very serious in maintaining law and order. So the people probably did not hang around long enough to finish the job on Paul.

Jesus, you will recall, told the witnesses who brought the woman to Him who had been caught in a capital crime, adultery, in so many words, that the one who was free of sin should cast the first stone. None of the witnesses cast a stone. We usually think that they felt guilty and that is why they did not do it. But it may be that they were afraid of what might happen to them under Roman law.

The Hebrews and other primitive cultures often invoked inanimate objects as witnesses. In Gen. 31:44 and 45 we are told that when Jacob left his father-in-law, Laban, they made a covenant between them. Jacob was to take good care of Laban's daughters and not bring harm to them or to him. Laban said, "Let us make a covenant, I and thou; and let it be for a witness between me and thee. And Jacob took a stone, and set it up for a pillar." A passage often quoted in relation to this incident which is beautiful when taken out of context but when in context has a totally different meaning is this, "The Lord watch between me and thee, when we are absent one from another." (Gen. 31:49) When taken out of context and used as we use it today it is meant in love and trust and the desire to give a blessing to someone for whom we care very much. Between Jacob and Laban there was not much love and probably very little trust. His father-in-law had tried to cheat him when they were dividing up the flocks. Jacob got a raw deal when he agreed to work for Laban in order to marry his first love, Rachel. Laban did not remind Jacob of the law that the oldest daughter had to marry first until after the incident and then Jacob had to work seven more years. So the covenant was made because they did not trust each other. In verse 52 of the same chapter we read, "This heap be witness, and this pillar be witness, that I will not pass over this heap to thee, and that thou shalt not pass over this heap and this pillar unto me, for harm." This passage itself tells us that the other above quoted passage was made out of a distrust of each other.

Literally this commandment means one should not lie about his neighbor, not only before judges or priests or before any other person. He should not say things that are derogatory about his neighbor and should not be a party to the spreading of damaging tales about other people. This was probably meant for those who were members of the Covenant Community. All kinds of things were probably said about people who were considered outsiders. You will remember that famous parable of Jesus about the Good Samaritan. A man asked Jesus, "Who is my neighbor?" It was quite a shock to him when Jesus went beyond the members of the Covenant Community and said those hated, half-breed Samaritans are your neighbors. Do not bear false witness against them but love them.

Sometimes when two people come together one will say, "What's new?" Then they get into a discussion of negative things that are going on in their lives and in the lives of others. In discussing someone they both know one of them may even say, "Do you have any juicy information about him or her?" When discussing or gossiping about another person they want to know what is bad more than they want to know of the good things the person may have done. It may be that the good may make them look bad.

Another way we might interpret this commandment for help today is this, "Do not bear or carry in your mind and heart, your thoughts and your feelings, your opinions, negative information about others," even if the information is based upon facts. According to appearances it may seem that someone is a hopeless and helpless critter. But according to the truth, that person is a child of God and very much loved by God. In fact God loves the negative appearing person as much as he loves the ones who seem to be saintly characters. We as humans might ask, "How can God love someone who does such horrible things?" That is one of the things that baffles the human ego. It is the nature of His love; it is unconditional. God does not love us because we are good; he loves us whether we are good or not. He knows that some day, somewhere along the pathway of life we will, like the prodigal son, come to ourselves. That means we will wake up out of the deep sleep of negative human consciousness and seek to return to a right relationship with God. Then we will know and understand and be very grateful that through all the time that we were out living on our own, doing as we pleased, God loved us and waited patiently for our return so that He could show us and teach us how to live in this great and wonderful universe without suffering and pain and fighting and hating and misery. He would show us how to live in peace and harmony, and how to experience even eternal life, not even suffering death.

The human ego finds it very challenging to think about others as God thinks about everyone. Just take for an example what the human ego may think about a character like Hitler and then ask how God thinks about Hitler. Do you think God hates Hitler as many humans hated and still hate him? You no doubt have heard individuals say, "I cannot bear the thought..." One who makes such a statement is admitting that just thinking about someone is a painful and unpleasant experience. Jesus said to His disciples, "I have yet many things to say unto you but ye cannot bear them now." (John 16:12) It would be too challenging to them, mentally and emotionally, if He had told them the complete truth. They were having difficulty accepting what He did tell them.

Take for example the statement He made, "Thou shalt love thy neighbour as thyself." They knew this from the Old

Testament law. Jesus was quoting Lev. 19:18 but He could see that they had a limited view about who the neighbor was. Even his own disciples found this to be challenging. Judas was probably not the only one of the twelve who was a zealot. It may be that even Peter was. After all he had a sword with him the night Jesus was arrested. He probably thought Jesus was going to start a revolution and he wanted to be ready to begin killing the hated Romans.

In thinking about this commandment we should bear in mind the high opinion that we have about ourselves is the same high opinion that we should bear or carry about others. The love that we have for ourselves, the willingness to forgive ourselves, the willingness to be kind to ourselves is the same willingness that we should have toward others. It may seem that some do not have a very high opinion of themselves but underneath it all they certainly do. Just observe their reaction if something derogatory is said to them or about them. They are quick to defend themselves. Defensiveness is an indication that a person does have a high opinion of himself but feels frustrated because he cannot or does not understand how to express this high opinion in successful ways.

There is another very important reason why this commandment is helpful. The thoughts we think about others have a decided effect upon us. The negative thoughts a person holds about another can make him miserable. These thoughts can cause him to do things that can be very damaging to him. The negative thought may lead a person to harm or even kill another person. The negative thoughts and emotions held in consciousness may have no effect upon the other person but for the one holding them they might make him ill. They can certainly destroy his peace of mind and happiness. The expression "I get so angry when I think of him" reflects the misery that a person experiences when he bears in his mind false testimony. Remember anything that is not the truth about another person is false testimony. The commandment, therefore, from the positive side would say, "Bear the truth about your neighbor."

And what is the truth? Your neighbor is first and foremost the image and likeness of God. He may not appear to be anywhere near Godlike. But remember appearances are not the truth. Appearances are the false information that we carry around in our minds, not only about people, but even about God and the rest of the universe. Jesus was making this point clear when He said, "Judge not according to the appearance, but judge righteous judgment." (John 7:24) Righteous judgment is discernment based on truth or principle, that which is eternal and never changes. Appearances are constantly changing and even at their best are limited.

In our religious theology we have been taught that human beings are basically evil or sinful. This is false testimony and is a violation of the ninth commandment. The concept of original sin as given over the years and the concepts of heaven and hell and that sinners will suffer eternal punishment is false testimony. Even though this is false testimony many continue to believe this and keep bearing it in their minds and hearts for many years, maybe thousands or even millions of years. Now is the time, if we can, to let go of this false testimony. Let us begin to bear the truth, to look beyond the outer appearances and actions and realize that the basic nature of every person is good. This has to be true if you accept the Biblical premise that all of us are created in the image and likeness of God. We are all in the process of rediscovering this basic truth about ourselves. That is what life is all about, to know who we are as spiritual beings.

With a growing awareness we discover things about ourselves and others that are incredible. We discover that we can do things we once thought were impossible. We discover talents and abilities we did not know we possessed. We discover that others also have the same great potential and that we are all equal. So, we not only need to cease bearing false witness against or about our neighbors, we need to cease bearing false witness about ourselves. No one as yet has realized his full potential. William James suggests that we are only utilizing about one tenth and that is a generous figure.

Take for example a simple task such as typing. You practice, and after learning some of the basics you get your speed up to twenty or twenty-five words a minute. If you keep on, you can increase that over one hundred percent. Some never utilize their possibilities in typing and stick to the hunt and peck system.

When I started running several years ago I could not even run one fourth of a mile without stopping and panting and gasping for breath. If I had accepted that as my limit I would still be doing that, but I did not stop there. It was quite a marvelous discovery to see how development could take place. I ceased bearing the false witness about the body. The day I was able to run one full mile was a thrilling and exciting experience. I kept on practicing and the day came when I could run seventeen miles without stopping. And the interesting thing about it is this. After running that long distance I was not as tired and gasping as I was when I only ran less than a mile in the beginning. What percentage of increase is that? About 1,700 percent. I am not telling this to get you to start running. I just mention it to show you that the great potential for increase is possible in any field of endeavor. But this increase is not possible if we bear the same old false witness of limitation.

Jesus came to tell us the good news; that is the meaning of the word Gospel. Some have caught the vision but many have not realized how good the news really is. Letting go of the false testimony opens the way for a higher, healthier vision of ourselves and others. It also helps us to realize this same truth so that we can bear the truth about others in spite of what they have done or are still doing.

When we start bearing the true witness about others it will change our whole philosophy about life. We will discover good things in them and about them that we never noticed before. We do not wait until they change, we are the ones that must change and we must change whether others ever do for the time being. Someday along the eternal pathway of life every human being will come to himself or herself as a son or daughter of God. They will come to the same realization about their divine relationship with God that Jesus had. That may be a challenging statement to make but Jesus is the one who assured us that it would be possible and I would rather take His word for it than the many misinformed followers who have been bearing false testimony all these years.

Jesus also said, "Ye shall know the truth and the truth shall make you free." (John 8:32) The truth will make or set us free from the false testimony so that we may truly become bearers of the light in our minds and hearts as well as in our actions.

The Tenth Commandment

Neither Shalt Thou Desire Thy
Neighbour's Wife, Neither Shalt Thou Covet
Thy Neighbour's House, His Field,
or His Manservant, or His Maidservant,
His Ox, or His Ass,
or Any Thing That is Thy Neighbour's.

De. 5:21

Out of all the commandments that deal with interpersonal relationships, this commandment deals with the inner attitudes of mind and heart, thought and feeling that one person may have toward another person. It is believed therefore to be a later addition to the total law code of the Hebrews.

It is in the consciousness of the individual where troubles usually begin. He often thinks that his troubles begin with some individual that may give him a difficult time or with some set of circumstances that he finds difficult to deal with or some other outer reason. He does not comprehend that his problem actually began with some negative thinking about the person or event. He has an experience or an encounter with someone, his passions or emotions are aroused in the form of resentment, hate, or some other violent way and in a negative, unillumined state of mind his human ego does not know how to handle the influence of his passions. It is very possible that his passions may be aroused in a so-called positive or pleasurable way and still he cannot handle them, he cannot control them, but lets them take charge and he follows their dictatory commands. This is the old story of Adam and Eve. The serpent, the information coming into the soul consciousness of the individual through his senses, makes promises or dictates commands; the passions are aroused in the form of excitement or overoptimistic expectation of easy gains, or in some negative way and Adam goes along with the influence of Eve, the passions.

When the passions are aroused by physical sights that seem pleasurable the individual thinks that anything pleasurable must be good. It makes him feel great at the moment and he sees no possible harm. In fact he may even convince himself with the reasoning mind that something so enjoyable and pleasurable can only be good and cannot possibly be harmful. We know today that this is not so. There are many pleasurable experiences that can be very detrimental, from sex to eating foods. This does not mean that they are totally bad but the excessive indulgence can be degenerating and may even lead to negative consequences. With all the research that is being done in sexual relations it is very easy to fall into the trap that such a pleasurable experience has no negative consequences. In fact some scientific investigators tout it as being a rejuvenating experience. There is much that we are not told, because the total experience is not considered, and by that I mean, what does it do to the physical body as far as energy and vitality consumption are concerned? What effect does excessive sexual indulgence have upon the mental capacities of the individual besides the temporary pleasure the individual experiences at the moment?

We know that eating is necessary for maintaining good health in the body. But we also know that overeating can be very damaging, for the effects of it put a great strain on all the organs of the body. It overworks the system and eventually the weak link breaks down and the individual has a health challenge. This applies to the pleasure one experiences from taking drugs and other stimulants that do not seem to be harmful because of the pleasure they seem to give; for example the continued use of drugs in foods that seem to be harmless such as caffeine in coffee and other beverages as soft drinks. Soft drinks are not as soft as we may think. They are so popular and it seems that the individual goes so long in consuming them that they seem harmless.

There are even harder drugs and stronger drinks that can lead to mental and emotional problems and physical challenges. We are all familiar with the effects of alcohol. Some seem to handle it very well whereas others have great difficulty with it. Even those who seem to handle it very well may be having problems, internally, that they are not aware of.

In the primitive state, the time when this commandment was given, the individual had very little self-control. We have not come very far from that state even today, for many have not learned to control their appetites, passions, and emotions. We are living in a very scientific age but we have sorely neglected the education and training of the inner man, the ego, the human personality.

What is covetousness? Webster says it is the wish one may have for something in an envious way. It is the desire to have and possess and experience something materially for the possible pleasure or gain that may come to the individual who is envious. At the time of Moses you will recall that the people, after leaving Egypt, spent some forty years wandering around in the wilderness. That must have been a very barren and unpleasant experience. Then all of a sudden they are brought into a land described as "flowing with milk and honey." It was such a beautiful and exciting experience for them. They saw all the gorgeous crops, fruits, nuts, animals, and other goodies and no doubt became very envious of the Canaanites. Many of the Hebrews became very wealthy but many of them remained very poor. Many believed they had no chance to enjoy or possess the wealth of the land and they probably sat around with strong, negative feelings of covetousness. In this envious state they were no doubt very greedy. Greed leads to violent actions to obtain the object desired.

Many battles and wars were fought as they tried to take possession of the land. They never did get the land completely even though they rationalized in their minds that God was giving it to them. It would seem that if God was giving it to them and if God was fighting their battles for them they would have been more successful. But as I have commented the promises of territory from the river of Egypt to Babylon were never fulfilled and no doubt never will be.

Greed was not only a problem of the poor at that time; it was also a problem for the rich. The rich wanted to be richer. There was much cheating, lying, coercing, and all the other negative things one may do trying to get in his possession the things that he covets. The people had not learned the principle that the later prophets taught and that Jesus stressed about true wealth. That principle was: GIVE AND YOU SHALL RECEIVE. They wanted to get without giving and that is an impossibility as far as obtaining true security and happiness.

One of the prophets of the Old Testament tried to get the point across when he said, "Bring ye all the tithes into the storehouse, that there may be meat in mine house, and prove me now herewith, saith the Lord of hosts, if I will not open you the windows of heaven, and pour you out a blessing, that there shall not be room enough to receive it." (Malachi 3:10) The "windows of heaven" are the windows of the mind. When we are open and receptive to God and look to Him for our supply He inspires or fills our minds with so many wonderful ideas that there is hardly room enough to receive and comprehend them. We cannot imagine how much good is in store for us. We get so fixed on possessing material things that we do not realize that those very material goods will be drawn to us without all the manipulation and effort that we usually put forth trying to get them through envy or other devious ways.

Covetousness is therefore an expression of lustful desire. Remember that lust is not only related to sex. As the commandment stresses, it was forbidden to desire or covet not only the neighbor's wife but all his other personal possessions, his land and animals as well. It is suggesting that one should not sit around with a negative desire for something that belongs to another, for that will only lead to frustration and trouble.

Philo, a Jew living in Alexandria during the time of Jesus, realized the possible danger of negative desire, lust, or covetousness and he wrote, "All the passions of the soul which spur and shake it out of its proper nature and do not let it continue in sound health are hard to deal with, but desire is hardest of all . . . For all the wars of Greeks and barbarians between themselves or against each other, so familiar to the tragic stage, are sprung from one source, desire, the desire for money or glory or pleasure. Those it is that bring disaster to the human race." (Philo, *Decalogue*) From this you can see that he is not saying that desire of itself is bad. It is the uncontrolled desire, expressed as covetousness, that leads to fighting. It gets the soul out of whack so to speak, what he calls the natural state and this affects the health of the individual.

Yes, desire is difficult to deal with. Rampaging, uncontrolled desire causes misery in an individual's life. This is a condition of the soul. It is not the things of the world that are bad and evil and must be denied. It is the covetous desire raging in the soul that must be tamed. It is very easy to get worked up. All we have to do is watch the reaction of people when they are on TV programs and are told that they have won a car or a large sum of money. They can hardly contain themselves. They jump up and down, hug and kiss the program leader; they cry, they shout, and some even scream.

It takes a great deal of discipline to control these emotions and that comes with many years of training and a proper understanding of the relationship between the soul and body. Both have the possibility of immortality, but not on the human level of understanding. The soul will always continue long after it leaves the body, for it is immortal even if it is untrained. The soul is very important but how much time do we devote to the training and discipline of the soul? How careful are we about the information that we put into the soul?

In general, more time is given to the development, pampering, training, and improvement of the body. This is good and I believe one should take time for bodily training, exercise and improvement. But I believe ten times as much time should be given to the training and development of the soul. I personally spend much more time reading and studying about spiritual laws, principles, and truths, than I spend in physical exercise. The physical part is important and I do spend time at that but I will never let it become the major part of my effort to have and experience the good life.

There is one thing that we must keep in mind and it is the great truth that the soul always controls the body. The body is an outpicturing of all the beliefs, attitudes, feelings, and emotions that we entertain in the soul. The body pictures our positive and negative beliefs. There is much we do not know about the body and therefore there is much soul training that needs to be done. If there is no soul cultivation or education in truth, then the body exerts a violent and dominating control over the individual. The individual, even the one with good intentions, gets involved in experiences that lead to physical health challenges. We should not automatically assume that all physical health problems are due to negative deeds. As I have stressed before many times, there are many instances when development leads to physical health challenges in the same way that the exercising of unused muscles very often makes the individual very sore. In fact it has been expressed that if after exercise you do not hurt, you did not exercise enough or at least not intensely enough.

We all want to have a good life of health, happiness and the material goods that make life comfortable and all these things are possible. They are much more possible than even we think. But they are not possible through greed and selfishness. One cannot become wealthy by cheating or taking or even desiring what belongs to others. One can only achieve the good of life through the proper development of his soul. He or she must learn to draw upon the great inner potential that is within the soul. That potential is God.

Desire is a soul quality. All desires must be controlled and must be under the direct influence of our indwelling Spirit. Notice that I say our indwelling Spirit, the Real Self and not just the ego self, what we refer to as the human spirit. In an unillumined soul state we labor under the delusion that if we get things we will fulfill the craving of the soul for happiness. But it does not work that way. The only thing that will lead to the good life is a knowledge of truth. This is more than a psychological formula for success. There are mental gimmicks that we can use to get a few material things but not the great blessings that are given freely and generously to us by God. There are no mental gimmicks that will give one peace of mind, happiness, and security. Those good qualities come only from a knowledge of universal law. The search for truth is a lifelong pursuit. Yet we take it too lightly. We think we can learn all there is to be known about metaphysical truths in a weekend or simply by reading one book. Study, as I have said, is important but it will take a great deal of it. We will have to read hundreds of books and spend many hours in lectures and classes, and many more hours in meditation to develop the true soul growth that will enable us to develop self-control and discipline our passionate nature.

The human ego does not want to spend this time but one day it will give up and give in and will be willing to let go and undergo the transformation process. The refining of the soul takes time, it takes effort, it takes struggle. This does not mean it is all hard work and no fun, for when one really realizes the growth that is taking place it will be one of the most pleasurable experiences he can have. This refining process will take place daily if the student is really sincere. If the student is just seeking quick, easy, fast, outer benefits or possessions he will be very disappointed. Over the years I have known of individuals who have not learned this lesson yet and they are still running to and fro looking for the secret formula for material gain and success. They will never find it, but they think they are being persistent and expressing faith by putting up a gallant effort. They are sticking to it even when the going is rough. They bolster themselves up with a lot of pacifying slogans. They really work at it as we so often hear in metaphysical circles. What they have not realized is that they do not have to work at it in the hard, difficult human way. The true idea is to let go and let God work through them.

Many fail to realize that it is soul improvement that improves our physical lot in life. Covetousness leads to frustration and that is one basic reason for this commandment. It is given not as a stern dictator would try to force us to do something against our will. It is given as a statement of principle to help us realize and experience the great good that is already prepared and waiting for us. A true relationship with God cannot be established as long as covetousness is active in the soul. It must be dealt with and put to rest.

And how do we do that? By realizing that first of all covetousness is based on a belief in lack and limitation. What one seems to envy or desire of another person's is not his possessions as such. What he simply wants to know is that he too can be equally blessed. God does not play Robin Hood with humanity. He does not take from the rich and give to the poor, for He does not have to. God is wealthy. Everything belongs to Him. With God there is more than enough of any good thing in life to satisfy the needs and desire of every human being. It is greed, selfishness, and covetousness that keep us from realizing the great wealth of God. Wars are fought over the meager goods that seem to be available while all the time there is much more good available than we can possibly use.

In human consciousness we think there has to be lack as an incentive for people to work and to do the things they do not want to do. This only reveals our limited knowledge and understanding. And this type of thinking is used as a rationalization to maintain vested interests and to hold on greedily and selfishly to what one may have. All this is now changing. We are entering into a new era in our social and economic structure where things are going to be quite different. Vested interests are being broken up and this is going to lead to greater good. It seems that today unemployment is a problem but in the future the real problem will be the positive side of unemployment, namely leisure. We are seeing today that many tasks can be done without human labor. These tasks are performed by robots which are more efficient and can actually do more work, faster work, and better work.

American industry has been shocked, startled, and surprised by the Japanese. The automobile industry thought it had a monopoly on the car market. They kept making cars in the same old way, gas guzzlers that were not efficient with their rear wheel drives. Along came the Japanese with their fuel efficient front wheel drive cars. The American automobile makers no doubt knew how to do all this but they probably did not want to spend the money to retool and begin making fuel efficient cars. Now they have lost a large portion of the market. According to the information given in the book, *Megatrends*, this will continue to happen in this country and one day most of our consumer goods will be produced by foreign countries.

This is not bad news; it is good news. It will challenge us to open up and become more receptive and willing to grow. We will make discoveries that will revolutionize our way of living. We will not think of unemployment but we will think in terms of leisure. And we will have to ask ourselves the question, "What will I do with all this extra leisure time that I have?" The time will come when the physical needs of the individual will be so easily and abundantly provided for that he will have to do one of two things. He will have to really get down to the serious business of studying truth and cultivating eternal soul values and qualities or he will look for further ways to stimulate his senses and have erotic pleasure and destroy himself. Will we use it wisely? Or will individuals be bored and frustrated over unfulfilled lustful desires? Will the individual find and discover that the search and discovery of truth is more joyous and rewarding? Soul pleasure will bring about outer sensual pleasure. But it will be a controlled sensual pleasure. The individual will know how to exercise self-control and when he says no to some sensual pleasure he will be able to mean it.

Soul pleasure comes when we have the knowledge to live in an exacting universe of law and order. The astronauts who go out in space and have one of the most thrilling adventures of their lives are obeying the laws of the universe. They are not out there doing what they might want to do. They do not just go outside the craft just to see what it is like. They know they have to function within their knowledge of the law. Some day there will be even bigger space craft that will take off from planet earth as easily as a modern day jet takes off from a local airport. The advent of the jumbo jet was quite a surprise for the average person. Who would have thought that such a huge aircraft could fly with so many people in the comfort that is provided? Well, in the future it will be even better than that.

The discoveries that are to be made out in space as well as the advancements here on earth are going to be even more astounding than anything we have known so far. I suppose one of the biggest and most astounding will be that not only individual but even national self-protection can be achieved very simply without huge outlays of money for military hardware and weapons. We will discover that no nation or group of people can intimidate others with their military might. No nation will be able to dictate to another nation how it shall live and function. In fact all military hardware will become useless and obsolete. We will discover a method, not just a technique, that will make this a glorious reality. This will be the real and true discovery of what truth and freedom are all about.

At the present time we are too satisfied, convinced, and settled in our human views of limitation about life. Many have lost their optimism. There are many prophets of doom to encourage us along the negative lines of thought. Complacency leads to decadence. When trust is awakened in the soul it makes us new creatures, new creatures with new power and ability. It will make us a new creature with a new vision about life and a new vision about ourself and our relationship with

God. We will know as did the Psalmist that God is our protection. There will be such a powerful forcefield emanating from the soul of the individual that he will literally be indestructible. Anyone who would seek to enter that forcefield would only destroy himself if he had destructive intentions.

The Bible tells us of these great possibilities. The prophet Isaiah was seeking to arouse the people, to lift their vision and expand their faith and optimism when he said to them, "Arise, shine; for thy light has come, and the glory of the Lord is risen upon thee." (Is. 60:1) This is what we need to do today. We need to rise out of the negative, covetous desires and realize that all good is possible not only for us but for everyone.

There is another beautiful passage given by Isaiah that reveals not only the protection that will be provided by God when the individual is receptive but tells us that we will be guided by a new light, the new light of an inward intuition. He said, "Violence shall no more be heard in thy land, wasting nor destruction within thy borders; but thou shalt call thy walls Salvation, and thy gates Praise. The sun shall be no more thy light by day; neither for brightness shall the moon give light unto thee: but the Lord shall be unto thee an everlasting light, and thy God thy glory. Thy sun shall no more go down; neither shall thy moon withdraw itself: for the Lord shall be thine everlasting light and the days of thy mourning shall be ended." (Is. 60:18-20)

This is such a beautiful passage and has such fantastic meaning. If it is read as outer phenomena we will miss the whole point. No destruction within the borders means within the soul. The great battles of the soul will come to an end for the individual will learn how to live harmoniously with all the laws of life. And that will be his Salvation. The sun and moon that have been gathering factual information and trying to live by that outer knowledge will no longer be necessary. The individual will be living by an everlasting light, the light from within, the inspiration that comes to us in the form of intuition or inner knowing. When that happens there will be no more mourning, no more intellectual and emotional discouragement.

Jesus has said and all true prophets have told us since His time that when the inner awakening takes place, great power and ability will be realized by the individual. We will be able to do the things that Jesus did. He will have power over life and death as Jesus had it. You may have thought that Jesus was put to death without His consent but that only revealed the limited thought of His followers. Jesus permitted the crucifixion to show to us the tremendous power He had. There was another occasion when the mob wanted to kill Him. They grabbed Him and wanted to take Him to the edge of a cliff and throw Him over and get rid of Him. When they got to the edge of the cliff Jesus was not there.

When Jesus stopped at Jacob's well and talked with the Samaritan woman, His disciples went into town to get some food. When they came back and offered Jesus some He said He had food to eat that they did not know about. They wondered what that food was and who gave it to Him. They did not know what Jesus was talking about. Jesus knew how to sustain His physical body without the necessity of eating food. Jesus did many astounding things and He said that all that He did we could do when we gained the understanding.

Jesus stood up one day in a synagogue and quoted a beautiful Old Testament passage that is still appropriate for us today. The passage reads, "The Spirit of the Lord God is upon me; because the Lord hath anointed me to preach good tidings unto the meek, he hath sent me to bind up the broken hearted, to proclaim liberty to the captives, and the opening of the prison to them that are bound; To proclaim the acceptable year of the Lord . . ." (Is. 61:1-2) Jesus always preached good tidings but His followers have not done so. They may have loved Him and they may have been sincere but they were totally misinformed about His great message. Even today the majority of His followers do not understand the full significance of what He had to say.

These words of Isaiah that I have just quoted are for those who are ready to open their minds to the great potential that is within them. They were true at Isaiah's time and they were true at Jesus' time, and they are true today.

We rise in consciousness through soul development and soul development takes place when we seek truth unselfishly, not with the selfish interest of material gains, benefits and the pursuit of pleasure. The real truth student does not have to be persuaded to seek truth by making promises to him of great material rewards, fame, fortune, or even health. The real truth student is one who has come to realize that he wants to know the truth for the truth's sake. The teacher does not have to promise him that he will become a millionaire overnight or that his problems will be solved immediately, that all his pain and suffering will be instantly alleviated. He does not have to try to manipulate God; he knows that cannot be done. He also knows that he cannot achieve or have anything until he has developed the consciousness in the soul that will produce it. Therefore, he will never try to get something for nothing. He will not live in the misery of covetousness for he knows that his own good will come to him when he is ready in consciousness.

The real truth student will know and understand what Jesus meant when He said, "Seek ye first the kingdom of God, and his righteousness; and all these things shall be added unto you." (Mat. 6:33) He knows that more good will be showered upon him than there will hardly be room enough to receive it.